Ballroom Dancing Is Not for Sissies
An R-Rated Guide for Partnership

ELIZABETH A. SEAGULL
ARTHUR A. SEAGULL

ISBN: 1-4392-1050-0

ISBN-13: 9781439210505

Visit www.booksurge.com to order additional copies.

For our parents: Eva and John, Frieda and Henry, whose love created us; and our children: David, Jacob, and Jon, whose love sustains us.

Be kind, for everyone you meet is fighting a hard battle.

Plato

Life isn't about waiting for the storm to pass...

It's about learning to dance in the rain.

Unknown

CONTENTS

Gold Level Relationship Fitness—Advanced Practice

BALLROOM DANCING IS NOT FOR SISSIES
An R-Rated Guide for Partnership

PREFACE

Art says: Actually, it was this book that saved our marriage—although Betty didn't know it at the time. We were at a dance competition. We had danced the American Smooth style, and I had danced the best I ever had. Not well enough to win, but the best I ever did. I felt great.

Then in two days I would be dancing the International Standard, which we had stopped practicing because we had been working so hard to learn our new smooth choreography.

Betty didn't have the time to rehearse with me—she was busy dancing pro-am Rhythm all day. The regulation size floor wasn't available because it was in use for the competition, and the practice floor was so small as to be pretty much useless for practicing Standard.

So what could I do to prepare? I did what any normal person would do—I had a panic attack. I *never* would remember the choreography! I made a plan: I would never interact with anyone again. I would become a hermit and live alone. I'd still be depressed, but at least it wouldn't matter, because I wouldn't be bothering anyone else. *Wait*—better still, I would join a monastery! I'd divorce Betty and never have to dance again, so I'd never have dance jitters again. The more I thought about this, the better it sounded. It would completely solve all my problems.

But then I thought about this book. Ten years' work, and it would ruin everything if I divorced Betty just before we published a book on improving your dance relationships. I'd be a laughingstock. I couldn't bear the shame.

So, you see, this book saved my, our, marriage. Who knows, maybe it can do the same for you...

Betty responds: You see what I'm up against? But we had to write this book because we needed it for ourselves. Just like you, we wanted to dance together to have fun, and then found ourselves having to confront our relationship issues in new ways. We thought of giving up dancing many times when the going got rough, but dancing together is a lot like marriage. While it may not always be a bed of roses, if we hang in there through the rough patches, we won't have to sleep on the thorns, and those luscious rose petals make it all worthwhile. Besides, we can't stop dancing now that dancing saved Art's life. You can read about that in Chapter 14.

Purpose

This book is about couple relationships. Specifically, it is about how to have a successful and satisfying dance partnership. Lots of couples decide to take dance lessons because they think it will be fun. But, at some point, they begin to find that dancing together is more challenging and stressful than they had expected. When this happens, a lot of couples drop out and stop dancing. Other dancers, even successful championship dance professionals, change partners when relationship issues get too heated. What a waste.

We believe it is possible to have it all—a happy and satisfying relationship and a compatible dance partnership. In fact, we believe that dancing can help couples with their relationship issues. Partnered dancing can be as life-changing or as superficial as you care to make it. We started out just like you—looking for fun, a way to have a "date" together one night a week by taking a dance class. Along the way we became fascinated by how much dancing appeared to intensify and reveal the psychological dynamics within each couple (including ourselves). Dancing seemed to do for adults what play therapy does for children—

give us an opportunity to play out our inner lives, including fears and wishes we don't know how to put into words.

Over time we discovered that dancing together forced us to face issues we might have preferred to avoid. Gradually, we developed a system for handling the conflicts that naturally arise in every dance partnership. Through using this system we learned to trust each other more and be more playful within our relationship. The result has been to deepen our emotional connection, improve our dancing, and lead us to having a lot more fun.

If you follow the recommendations in this book, we think you can do this, too. You don't have to choose between your dancing and your relationship—you can have both!

We also need to tell you what this book is *not*. This is not a book to teach you how to dance. There are no instructions here on dance steps or choreography. No one can learn that from a book. If you want to learn to dance, you need to take lessons from a competent dance professional. This book is also not a substitute for marriage counseling. If your relationship is in serious trouble, you need to work on it with a trained therapist.

Audience

This book is for adults who want to dance with a partner. If you dance by yourself, your errors are your own problem. But as soon as you dance with a partner, what you do affects another person, just as their mistakes affect you. Since you are both human, you will both make mistakes. What happens then will impact both your dancing and your relationship.

Why do we say this is a book for adults only? Because children who are learning to dance really don't have to deal with the kind of relationship issues adults face in their dance partnerships.

Sure, they may get mad at each other, and no doubt they could benefit from learning the **3Rs** at a "junior" level. But they do not have to deal with the deeper issues of sexuality, boundary violation, trust, and shame that can seriously complicate adult dance partnerships.

Why do we say ballroom dancing is not for sissies? Because it takes deep commitment and courage to stick it out and work through the issues that often surface in dance partnerships.

Amateur dancers are the primary audience for this book, but professional dance couples will benefit, as well. It's hard to portray harmony on the dance floor if you are fighting in rehearsal.

Dance teachers also need this book. It will help you understand your students, as well as helping you understand yourself. If you are experienced, you already know that the better dancers get, the more important the psychological issues become in determining performance outcomes. It was dance pros who first asked us to write this book. "We know how to teach dancing," they said, "but the couple issues keep getting in the way. We're not trained to deal with that!"

Anyone who participates in a coupled sport, such as ice dancing or even doubles tennis, can also benefit from the principles in this book for establishing and maintaining a harmonious partnership.

Organization

In Chapter 1 we explain in detail the problem that caused us to write this book. The rest of the book is organized around the solution, a system of relationship fitness based on the **3Rs**: respect, responsibility, and responsiveness. These, in turn, are organized into levels that correspond to dance levels: bronze, silver, and gold.

After Chapters 2–4, which set out the basics of the **3Rs** at the bronze level, Chapter 5 gives guidelines for taking care of your body. Chapter 6 shows you how to apply the **3Rs** to the "dance spat." Chapters 7–9 then take the **3Rs** to the silver level, exploring the taboo areas of sex and power in the dance partnership, as well as frankly discussing the weird experience we all have of wanting to learn while also, at times, wanting to kill our teacher.

Chapter 10 gives detailed guidelines for applying the **3Rs** in performance and competition. We also share many practical tips we have learned over the years to help you prepare for performing and competing, including advice on grooming, packing, and controlling performance jitters.

Chapters 11–13 take the **3Rs** to the gold level of relationship fitness. Finally, in Chapter 14 we review and summarize what we have learned and discuss how you can apply these skills to your relationship outside the dance. There are two bonus sections at the end of the book: a Partnership Compatibility Questionnaire to help you choose a dance partner whose interests and goals are compatible with yours; and Some Basic Principles of Human Learning as Applied to Teaching Dance to help dance teachers become more effective in the difficult job of teaching adults to dance.

Terminology

We use the terms "lady" and "gentleman" as well as "woman" and "man" to describe members of the dance partnership. Although speaking of "ladies and gentlemen" is rather old-fashioned, it is traditional to refer to ballroom dancers in this way. It is our hope that using these old-fashioned terms may promote respectful behavior among dancers.

We are, of course, aware that same-gender couples may dance together. In fact, it is necessary for the teacher to dance with everyone as part of the instruction, so two men or two women dancing together is something that happens every day in a dance studio. Our use of gender-specific language is not intended to slight same-gender couples. College competitions have tried to avoid gender-specific language by using the terms "leader" and "follower," but we have a different problem with that—we believe that both members of the couple take turns leading and following (see Chapter 4).

So we have gone ahead and used gender-specific language in many places. We hope that you, the reader, will understand that in some cases the woman's part may be danced by a man, and vice versa.

There are two other terms that we use interchangeably: teacher and coach. Both of these terms refer to someone who is more highly qualified than you who is teaching you how to dance, or how to improve your dancing. Amateurs usually refer to their dance "teacher," while professionals tend to receive "coaching." But, as we explain in Chapter 8, sometimes a studio brings in an outside "coach" to teach the amateurs and the pros. So you may have both a teacher and a coach. And you may have more than one teacher or coach.

Acknowledgments

So many people have given us ideas that made their way into this book. It is impossible to thank them all. We want to thank the people who first taught us to dance: Lisa King, Amy DeMellio, and Terry Worrall. Many of the stories in this book are derived from events we experienced and observed in their classes.

Our profound thanks to Louis Soma, the teacher/coach who has worked with us the longest and Betty's pro partner. He not only taught us to dance, he believed in us and supported us through many ups and downs as we grappled with the issues described in this book. His teaching is deeply psychological, as well as a lot of fun. He is a brother and a friend.

We also want to acknowledge the many coaches we have had private lessons with over the years: Pierre Allaire, Glenis Dee Creger, Rickey Geiger, Julia Gorchakova, Shirley Johnson, Joe Lozano, John Neymchek, Enrique Ramon, Esther Rehm, Kathryn Schaffer, Forrest Vance, Mirelle Veilleux, and, most of all, Rosendo Fumero. We have learned so much from each of them. Rosendo has been our main coach and choreographer for more than ten years. We so greatly appreciate the beautiful choreography he gives us, as well as the encouragement, wisdom, and inspiration he provides.

We have also benefited enormously from the many group coaching sessions we have attended over many years from top dance professionals too numerous to mention here. We gain valuable new insights from every hour spent learning from the best dancers in the business.

We are extremely grateful for all the encouragement that we have received from everyone in the dance community to write this book, from our dear friend, Judy Susskind (the loudest voice in ballroom cheering); to music vendor Rick Popp, who constantly asked, "Have you two written that book yet?"; to Sam Sodano, owner of the Ohio Star Ball, who is always ready to do anything that will help promote ballroom dancing. We cannot thank him enough for his support and encouragement over the years.

Our conversations with Judy Wright, Dance Editor at Human Kinetics, helped us sharpen our ideas about what kind of a book this should be. We appreciate her guidance. Earlier versions of the manuscript benefited greatly from helpful critique by Nancy Compton and Judy Smith. We thank our friends, Murry and Jerry Perlmutter, for the original version of the responsiveness exercise in Chapter 4. We are grateful to Donald Kaufman, MD, for reading and correcting an earlier version of Chapter 5. We appreciate suggestions from Stephen Yelon, Professor Emeritus of Education, on Some Basic Principles of Human Learning as Applied to Teaching Dance. We are most grateful for Diane Levy's corrections to the manuscript. Her editing has been both sharp-eyed and gentle.

Despite all the help we have received from others, we know that nothing is perfect, and this book is no exception. Therefore, there are bound to be a few errors that managed to slip by everyone. For these we, the authors, take full responsibility.

Ballroom Dancing Is Not for Sissies

Chapter 1

ARE WE HAVING FUN YET?

The Problem

Ah, ballroom dancing, so romantic, so passionate, so…

"Get OFF me you oaf!"

"Well if you would FOLLOW!"

Sound familiar? Dancing is supposed to be fun. Yet conflict between dance partners is common. Why? What happens to prevent dancing from being a natural, joyful activity?

Joyful Dancing

We were camping in the Sahara Desert. The moon was full. The stars glittered in the clear, cool night sky. Erg Chebbi, the mother of all dunes, loomed dimly above us. As we sat around the crackling campfire, tall figures swathed in robes of blue materialized out of the darkness. Tuareg nomads, descended from an ancient desert people, began to clap, sing, and drum. Our drivers and guides caught up whatever was handy—pots and spoons, an empty olive oil jar, an old water can, and joined in. Their feet and bodies moved to the music. Before long we, the foreigners from the West, began to join in the dance around the campfire, smiling and turning, laughing and leaping on the hard sand.

We did not understand the Berber language of the songs they sang, and the tunes were unfamiliar, but we were united in that magical moment in time by the universal language of rhythm and ecstatic movement. It was a peak experience.

The feeling of joy that filled us that night is the feeling we all search for when we dance. Every now and then we get a small taste of it—even beginners feel it—only to lose it again. The desire to re-experience that addictive sensation (which psychologists call "flow"—see Chapter 13) is a powerful force that keeps us dancing, pushing on in the face of disappointments, obstacles, and even injuries.

Why was it so easy to be spontaneous and joyful in our desert dance? What were the psychological differences that set it apart from a social dance experience at home?

Well, for one thing, we had no expectations of what this dance should be like. It wasn't a waltz or a cha cha—there were no "dance figures" to get in our way. We simply expressed whatever we felt as we moved to the music.

For another thing, we were unselfconscious. We did not know these people and would never see them again. We did not care what they thought of us, so we were freed from any worry over what kind of an impression we were making. We did not judge ourselves or feel judged.

Finally, although in one sense it was a shared experience, in another sense each of us was dancing alone. As long as we didn't crash into each other or fall into the campfire, we did not have to maintain an awareness of coordinating our movements with those of any other dancer. We could do as we pleased.

> Work like you don't need the money.
> Love like you've never been hurt.
> Dance like nobody's watching.
>
> *Satchel Paige*

Reflecting on the conditions which made it so easy to dance joyfully in the Sahara helps us understand what gets in the way of capturing and hanging on to that wonderful feeling of joy when we are dancing at home. Dancing in the desert we had no anxiety about knowing particular dance figures, no self-consciousness about performance, and no concern about how to coordinate our movements with a partner. Apprehension, concern, self-consciousness—whatever you want to call it—are all variations on the theme of anxiety. This is the feeling that can rob us of pleasure in partnered dancing, or even prevent us from trying at all. But why do we feel anxious?

If we want to dance with a partner we must have some training that will allow us to coordinate our movements with theirs. And as soon as we get into a training situation something interesting happens to us.

The Dance Lesson

Bob and Carol go to their first lesson, a group class. Unsure of what to expect, and a little apprehensive, they stand around waiting to begin. Before long the teacher starts the class by announcing that she will play some music so that students can "warm up." Some couples begin to dance a little. Bob and Carol begin to worry. It looks like some of these people already know how to dance. "That's not fair, this is a class for beginners!" they think. "We are going to look like fools next to them!"

What they do not realize is that some of these couples have taken the class before…

Isn't it odd? On the first day of kindergarten we didn't think we were already supposed to know how to read, we knew we were there to learn. But when we go to a dance lesson, we somehow think this is a skill we should already have.

After the warm-up, the teacher has everyone line up and instructs them to walk forward, back, and to the side. Then she tells them they already possess the basic skills needed for dancing. "If you can walk, you can dance." This is reassuring. OK. We can walk, so we will learn to dance.

The first lesson isn't too bad. Everyone learns the basic waltz box, "forward side close, back side close."

The second lesson also begins with warm-up music. Bob and Carol decide to try the box they learned last week, but it is hard to figure out how to move without getting in each other's way. They notice that some couples seem able to move around the room, while their box doesn't go anywhere. They are amazed at how little they remember. Bob isn't sure which foot to start on, so Carol helps him by telling him. He can't feel the music, either, so Carol counts the beat out loud for him. He feels inexplicably angry about this help, but Carol feels better. They have trouble closing their feet, so they stop and watch another couple who seem to know how to do this. By the time the teacher begins, they are already getting discouraged.

The teacher reviews the box; then she teaches two new figures, a progressive step and an underarm turn. This feels like an awful lot of material to master. And how do you switch from one pattern to the other?

By the third lesson, couples have begun to drop out. Actually, this is an advantage for Bob and Carol, because it means they can get more individual attention from the teacher, but they don't realize this yet. The teacher asks Bob to volunteer to be her partner as she demonstrates a beginning rumba step. "Ohmigod," he thinks, "another dance? I don't know the waltz yet!"

He doesn't want to dance in front of everybody, but the teacher is young and attractive. She seems lively and fun, and wears short skirts and high heels. Bob feels he can't refuse. Although he feels like a klutz, when they finish the teacher tells him he has done very well, and has the class applaud for him. Bob begins to feel better. He realizes he had no trouble leading the teacher, so it must be Carol's fault when the dancing doesn't work. Carol begins to feel miserable. On the way home, Bob and Carol have a fight over whether he is doing his share of the housework.

Self-Consciousness, Expectations, and Oh Yes, My Partner

So what happens to us during a dance lesson? Why does the trouble begin when we have to focus on learning the dance steps and the technique necessary to execute them?

The answer is not surprising. Whether in group classes or private lessons, we begin to experience ourselves as inadequate. We are used to being reasonably competent at what we do—we are, after all, adults. We know how to drive a car, balance our checkbook, and hold down a job. How hard can it be to learn to dance? We expect to learn it quickly. But we seem to be learning dancing slowly—especially if we come to this as adults with no background in dance. Something about this feels confusing. The instructions seem simple enough, but we don't seem able to coordinate all our body parts. We don't know where our feet are. Our posture is incorrect. Instead of feeling like play, dancing begins to feel like work.

We begin to worry about what others will think of us. We become sensitive to criticism. And if someone tries to help us, we defend ourselves, which interferes with our learning.

At the same time, a more mature part of ourselves realizes that our attitude has unexpectedly become rather childish and self-defeating, so we become angry with ourselves. Then we are even more sensitive to the imagined judgments of others because we are already harshly judging ourselves. So we deflect criticism from ourselves by attacking someone else. The partner is the safest and handiest target. "*You* are doing the step wrong. If you would do your part right, I could do my part right. You are preventing me from being a good dancer." Or, conversely, "Well I just can't learn this as fast as you. I'm a klutz. I'm hopeless. I might as well quit. You'll never want to dance with me."

And all this happens so fast that we don't even see it coming until we are in the middle of it. Much of it takes place just outside of consciousness, because our conscious focus is on the content of the lesson. When the anger and frustration break through, it is too late. We must hunker down into our position to defend it or risk feeling even more ridiculous.

Dancing Assaults Our Defenses

The truth is that partnered dancing is an activity that tends to assault psychological defenses. All of us have psychological defenses; indeed, we need them. Defenses help us manage the anxieties of everyday life. Without being aware of it, we all construct and refine our defenses over time in response to problems that arise in the course of our development. We use our defensive system, with greater or lesser success, to reassure ourselves that we are OK, to get through the day, and to do what has to be done.

In normal social interactions people observe an unspoken agreement: don't notice my defenses and I won't notice yours. We call this a nonaggression pact. The close physical contact and movement involved in dancing, however, expose what is otherwise hidden. We are suddenly thrown back into a less mature version of ourselves. If we have the courage to look into our inner self when this is happening, instead of defending, distracting ourselves, and running in the opposite direction, we may be surprised as we discover the "leftovers" from earlier stages of development.

> ## Nothing is more revealing than movement.
> *Martha Graham*

Everyone's "leftovers" are slightly different, depending on the life experiences they have had, but they all involve worries about whether we will be able to live up to the expectations we have of ourselves and how we will be judged by others. In dance situations, these concerns most commonly take the form of:

- unrealistic perfectionism, and
- a desire to blame others for mistakes.

Perfectionism

When you were in second grade you could study for the spelling test and if you worked hard, you could get 100 percent. If you made your bed neatly every morning, you could please your mother. If you did all your chores properly and without fussing, you might earn your allowance, get a treat, or, in some families, avoid a beating. Regardless of the details of life in any particular family, we all had childhood experiences that taught us we should try to be perfect.

Perfection, we grew to believe, meant love and approval from adults. Perfection may also have meant jealousy and resentment from siblings and peers, which made it more complicated. Perhaps it was not good to be too good. But experiences of failure brought external criticism and internal feelings of misery. "You aren't applying yourself." "You are disappointing your family." "You are lazy." "You could do better." "You are not living up to your potential."

And these are mild comments compared to what some of us received as children. So despite our adult achievements, all of us have little pockets of self-doubt and little corners of vulnerability where we are easily wounded. And bound up with all of this is the unexamined idea, left over from childhood, that perfection is not only desirable, it is actually possible. To put this in perspective, consider the batting average in baseball.

The Batting Average

The "batting average," a central concept in rating baseball players, expresses the ratio of successful hits per times at bat. Batting 1.000 means that the player gets a hit every time at bat. This has never been achieved! In fact, the average major league player only gets a hit once every four times at bat, a .250 batting average. A batting average of .333 is championship level—it will get a player into the Baseball Hall of Fame.

But this championship level means the batter gets on base only once in three tries—failing two out of three times. Yet when we are learning to dance, how many of us, at all levels, think we must be successful 100 percent of the time?

Such an impossible standard of perfection is a guarantee of disappointment. Does this mean we should not try to improve? Of course not. We all want to get better. But letting go of our unrealistic perfectionism can help us be more kind and forgiving of ourselves and our partners when we are less than perfect.

Dancing is playful—if we turn it into work, we lose its essence. Professional dancers, especially, have to watch out for this. Top sports figures know this: if you play for your work, you still have to keep it playful.

> I never had a job. I always played baseball.
>
> *Satchel Paige*

The Receding Horizon

We were hiking in the Badlands of South Dakota, a strange and uneven terrain, filled with beautiful colored rock formations. Over us was a bright blue sky. A hot sun beat down. Every time we clambered up to the next plateau, we thought we would be at "the top" where we would see a vast view over the land. But at the top of every rise our view was of more uneven terrain leading to the next plateau. After hiking a long time, we realized this was not like a mountain. There was no "top." There was always just more of the type of terrain we had already hiked. "Here" was very similar to "there." The horizon just kept receding.

Some friends of ours had been working hard at their dancing. Finally they passed the full bronze exam and were ready to begin learning the silver syllabus. When they went to the studio for their first silver lesson, they were shocked to discover that their teacher wanted to work on their Cuban motion. "What?" they thought. "We already did this!" They had expected that once they "made it" to the silver level they were finished working on the things they had learned at the bronze level. Instead of being at the "top," they found themselves at a new plateau.

After our first couple of years taking lessons, a relative was surprised to hear that we were still studying dancing. "You're still taking dance lessons? Haven't you learned it by now?"

At some point each of us discovers that dancing is a receding horizon. There is no point at which we have finished learning.

The best dancers *in the world* keep on taking coaching, trying to improve their technique.

> You may be disappointed if you fail, but you are doomed if you don't try.
>
> *Beverly Sills*

The shock of realization when we reach this moment in our dancing can help us grow up. We can begin to let go of perfectionism in other areas of our lives, as well. We don't have to blame our partner or ourselves. Perfection is impossible. But improvement is always possible, as long as we are willing to keep trying.

Blame

The other half of perfectionism is blame. Life is not perfect. It never has been and it never can be. Even if nothing is going drastically wrong, there is always the potential for things to be a bit different than we expect. We can either accept this reality, and learn how to make it work for us, or become more rigid and insist that life must conform to our preconceived ideas. The more closely we are wedded to the image in our heads of what "*should*" be, instead of accepting and embracing the reality that *is*, the more disappointed and angry we are likely to be. And the more we are disappointed and angry, the more we will look for someone to blame—either ourselves (the depressive position) or someone else (the angry position). Neither of these options is very helpful, and neither tends to increase the quotient of fun in life.

> Life is not the way it's supposed to be. It's the way it is.
>
> The way you deal with it is what makes the difference.
>
> *Virginia Satir*

Defense is the natural response to blame. Therefore, blame in any relationship will tend to activate the defenses of the person being blamed. Instead of a constructive conversation, which might result in solving a problem, an attitude of blame produces a mini-war. Attack and defense. What a waste of time and energy in a dance partnership! If a dance partnership is to succeed, the partners must constantly remember that they are on the same team. Teammates help each other. Blame helps no one.

The Practice Session

Ted and Alice have been taking dance lessons and begin to realize that if they don't practice on their own they tend to forget a lot of what they learn each week. They figure they can save money on dance lessons by practicing on their own—then they won't have to spend so much time reviewing every time they meet with their teacher. They belong to a gym, so they arrange to use space there.

Armed with dance shoes and a boom box for music, they begin to practice their waltz figures. Within the first three minutes, Alice complains, "You're pushing me!" "No, I'm not. I'm hardly touching you!" Ted says. "Well, to me *this* is a push!" says Alice, giving him a little shove. They try again. "But you don't *go* if I don't do what you call pushing!" says Ted. "Well,

I can't tell when you want me to go to promenade, but I don't want to be pushed, either," Alice retorts.

"Why don't you do it the way the teacher showed you? I don't have any trouble feeling it from *him*, but *he* doesn't push." "So you're saying it's *my* fault you don't move?" Ted angrily replies. "Other ladies seem able to follow me. Maybe it's you!"

This practice session is going nowhere fast. If Ted and Alice can't figure out how to practice without blaming each other, they will either stop dancing or look for a different partner. But if they are blaming each other when they dance, they are probably doing it in other areas of their lives, so giving up dancing will not solve the problem, it will only help to hide it.

Changing partners isn't the answer, either. The habit of blame will simply be carried into the new partnership, with another version of the same fight being played out. Without a system for handling the conflicts that are guaranteed to arise in the course of dancing, couples will destroy their dancing—or their relationship. So what can be done?

The Solution

Every dance couple needs a method for managing the conflict that rears up when defenses are threatened. The rest of this book teaches you a practical method that will:

- prevent many relationship conflicts from occurring, and
- teach you how to deal constructively with them when they do happen.

We call this method the **"3 Rs of Relationship Fitness: Respect, Responsibility, and Responsiveness."** By studying and applying the principles in the **3 Rs of Relationship Fitness**, couples can improve their dance partnership as well as all of their relationships. With a better relationship you will not only have more fun dancing, you will also learn faster and practice more effectively, because you will not be wasting time and energy on destructive interactions that interfere with pleasure and learning.

We have organized relationship skills in levels that correspond to levels of skill in dancing, but *dance* skill level and *relationship* skill level may be quite different. For example, a gold or advanced level dancer might be at the bronze level in terms of relationship skills. Therefore, you may find it useful to go through all the levels methodically, beginning with bronze and working your way up as you acquire new relationship fitness skills at each level. If you are one of those people who like to begin in the middle, you will still find this book useful. However you read it, we suggest returning to sections at earlier levels whenever you need review.

The next three chapters present the bronze level of the **3 Rs of Relationship Fitness**. As in dancing, bronze level skills are foundational skills—basics to which we must keep returning even as we progress through higher levels. When you move from bronze to silver in dancing, you do not abandon what you learned at the bronze level; you build on it. Just as with dance skills, when you move to the silver level of relationship skills, you don't leave bronze-level skills behind. There is a constant need to return to the basics and review them, even while you work on higher levels of skill.

Following the bronze level chapters on the **3 Rs** is a chapter on a fourth "**R**"—"**Reality Check**"—which refers to your physical status and bodily needs. A dancer is an athlete, so your tools must include attention to physical reality issues such as hydration, rest, and stretching. Chapter 6 then takes the foundational skills of relationship fitness and shows you how to apply them to a "dance spat."

At the silver level, there are again separate chapters on each of the **3 Rs: Respect, Responsibility, and Responsiveness**. Here we teach skills for handling some of the more complex issues that affect relationship fitness: developing a respectful approach to dancing and romancing, taking active responsibility for learning, and recognizing and dealing constructively with power issues in the dance partnership. Chapter 10 then shows you how to apply the relationship skills you have learned at the bronze and silver levels in the challenging arena of performing and competing.

Finally, Chapters 11 through 13 teach gold-level relationship skills. Again, just as top performers constantly return to practicing fundamental dance skills, bronze and silver level relationship skills are not abandoned. Rather, they are built upon to achieve the highest levels of relationship: radical respect for reality, openness to criticism, and achieving peak experiences of shared flow. Chapter 14 reviews what you have learned about personal growth and relationship fitness so that you can take these skills into your life beyond the dance, deepening and improving all your connections with others. Yes, it is true—by mastering and applying relationship fitness skills you will not only improve your dance partnership, you can improve all your relationships, leaving you happier and more successful in relating to others than you have ever been.

So let's get started! Shall we dance?

Bronze Level Relationship Fitness—
Foundations

Chapter 2

BRONZE LEVEL RESPECT: STAND UP AND SMILE

Respect Yourself

To hold your own in a dance partnership—or in any relationship—you must first respect yourself. Then you must learn to project your positive attitude physically. Your teacher will help you. Even if you have been to only one dance lesson, you already know that the first thing taught is posture—stand up and smile!

Exercise: Practicing Posture and Self Respect

Stand without shoes with your feet comfortably apart, but under your body. Take a long, deep breath, allowing your spine to lengthen. As you exhale, continue to lengthen your spine. Picture the spaces between the vertebrae opening up, little by little. Imagine how beautiful your bones are. Allow yourself to feel amazed by the wonder of the human body. Take another slow, deep breath and picture a string attached to the crown of your head. Floating at the end of the string above you is a beautiful red helium balloon. As you slowly exhale, picture the balloon gently tugging the crown of your head upward. Take a third slow deep breath and allow your shoulders to float downward as your spine remains lengthened. Slowly exhale and smile. Experience the comfortable lightness of your ribcage floating above your hips. Experience the pleasure of your smile.

You can do this exercise as many times as you like, with your eyes open or shut. You can do it before you begin to dance, in the middle of a lesson, at the end, or at times when you are not dancing. The more you practice this, the easier it will become to quickly recapture the positive feelings and good posture associated with it.

When you have good posture you feel better about yourself and your place in the world. As you straighten your spine you "lay your burden down." With good posture, your body says, "Here I am." As you experience yourself in your body, lengthening your spine and breathing deeply, you feel and project self-respect. Your smile is the outward sign of your inner pleasure.

The physical and the mental mirror each other. Interestingly, change can come from either side of this mirror. Although it is obvious to most of us that we smile when we feel good, many of us do not realize that we can actually improve our mood by smiling. Similarly, the way we hold our bodies as we sit or stand simultaneously creates and reflects how we feel about ourselves. That sense of self is projected out into our social world, where others unconsciously read and respond to our nonverbal cues. Try walking in a "pulled up" good dance posture in your "normal" life. You will be amazed at the reaction. People will turn and look at you. Others may not recognize you. When your posture is unusually good, you project something different into the social world, and people take notice.

Traditionally, dancing was taught as part of an array of social graces that had to be mastered, at least at a basic level, in order for people to function in polite society. This idea still has a lot to recommend it. Creating and projecting respect for oneself and others, skills that are fundamental to successful dancing, are social skills that never go out of style.

Use Positive Self Talk

So stand up straight and smile. Then match your good posture and open smile with a positive attitude. You can create and reinforce your positive attitude by practicing positive self-talk. Tell yourself: "I am here to enjoy myself." "This will be fun." "I can learn this. I *will* learn this."

Whenever you get discouraged, beware of negative internal messages. Monitor yourself and interrupt whenever you notice yourself saying internally, "What a fool I am." "Other people are learning this faster." "I have two left feet." "I feel like a klutz."

Never say these things out loud. The more you repeat negative messages, the more they affect you. (OK, you can tell your therapist or a trusted friend—but only to blow off steam when you are upset. Just don't let negative messages become a mantra. Are you over it now? Good. Breathe and smile.) Once you have pulled yourself together, replace negative self-talk with positive self-talk, both internally and externally. Try to make this your new habit. Improved posture and a more positive mental attitude will be only the first of the many unexpected benefits of learning to dance.

> Whether you think you can or think you can't—you are right.
>
> *Henry Ford*

Be Kind to Yourself

Dancing is a motor skill that is learned largely through repetition. Being "smart" isn't all that helpful. The seeming frequency of our errors and what feels like the slowness of our learning can come as a rude shock. But focusing on the negatives only distracts us from learning and slows us down even more. So respect yourself and treat yourself with kindness and compassion. This means no internal name-calling and no beating yourself up just for being human!

Part of respecting yourself and being kind to yourself is to respect the fact that you are doing this at all! Every dance teacher has stories about students who schedule their first lesson, and then don't show up. Or park in the parking lot and can't come in! Something about this activity is both attractive and very frightening for a lot of people. But you came through the door and stayed!

Over the years we have had many conversations with both friends and strangers that reflect the combination of longing and intimidation that people feel about dancing. For example:

Woman to Betty, "I wish I could dance like you!"

Betty, "You can learn. Why don't you take lessons?"

Woman, "I don't have a partner."

Betty, "You don't need a partner. You can dance with a teacher. Lots of women do that. I'll give you my teacher's card, if you like. His name is Louis Soma. He's a lot of fun and an excellent teacher."

Woman, "Oh, no, I couldn't. I'm not graceful like you."

Another variant on this conversation goes something like this:

Woman, "Oh, you're so lucky to have a husband who will dance with you!"

Betty, "Won't your husband dance with you?"

Woman, "Well, we took dance lessons once but we forgot everything."

Betty, "Yes, it's hard to remember it if you don't keep dancing. Why don't you take another class?"

Woman, "After the beginning class I wanted to take the intermediate class, but my husband said he wasn't ready—he wanted to take the beginning class over again, but I said I had already learned all that, so we just quit."

Yes, people envy you. They want to dance, but they are afraid. You, on the other hand are getting out there and trying. Good for you! That is truly something to respect about yourself.

Respect Your Partner

Self-respect is the first requirement, but in partnered dancing, respecting your partner is almost as important. Since respect is the foundation of any positive relationship, do not choose as a dance partner anyone you feel you can't respect. Choosing a partner for skill level alone is a mistake. If you have a low opinion of the person as a human being, you will not be able to enjoy dancing with him or her over time. Eventually, your lack of respect for your partner will take its toll and the partnership will end in ruin. (See the **Partner Compatibility Questionnaire** at the end of this book that you can take with a prospective partner to see whether you are a good match for each other.)

> Respect for ourselves guides our morals; respect for others guides our manners.
>
> *Lawrence Sterne*

Dance with someone whose company you enjoy, whether it is the love of your life or a casual acquaintance. Then treat your partner with good manners. Greet your partner cheerfully when you arrive at the lesson or practice. Make eye contact. Smile.

Speaking to your partner in a cheerful, upbeat manner when you first meet him or her upon arrival at the practice or dance venue is a comparatively easy skill, but it is an important one to cultivate, as it helps to set the tone for the interactions to follow. Don't overlook the easy stuff. There are enough things about dancing that are hard to do!

> ### Exercise: Practicing Respect for Your Partner
>
> Look your partner in the eyes when s/he arrives. Smile. Say, in a cheerful tone of voice: "Hello, partner (or use their name). How are you today?"
>
> Listen to their answer. Reply in a positive and supportive way. If they say they got stuck in traffic and it took forever to get to the studio, resist the temptation to say, "You think you have troubles? Just listen to what happened to me!" Instead, say, "Oh, you poor dear. I am sorry that happened to you," or, "Yes, the traffic can be such a problem at this time of day." Then move on with something upbeat, "But I'm so glad you are here now, safe and in one piece so we can practice!" Or, "I've been looking forward to seeing you." Or, "Isn't this fantastic weather we're having?"
>
> Remember that your goal is to show interest in and respect toward your partner. Find something about which you can give an honest compliment. "Nice slacks." "Your hair looks good today." Notice what your dance pro does in this regard and model these behaviors. Often the pros are very good at this.
>
> If your partner is someone with whom you are in a love relationship, you can do more, hugging and kissing upon greeting. You might want to give a bigger compliment, "What a good-looking partner I have. Am I lucky!" "I can't wait to dance with you!"
>
> Then get a drink of water and begin to move into your stretching routine.

Warm-Up

Many dance couples begin a practice session by stretching and then doing a separate warm-up before coming together to dance as a couple. Professional couples often do their separate practice for quite some time before coming together to dance.

We read that Baryshnikov typically stretched for four hours before a performance! (More about stretching in Chapter 5.)

Regardless of whether you warm up separately first, you will need to warm up as a couple to get used to the feeling of orienting and moving your bodies in response to each other. In keeping with the theme of respecting self and partner, during the warm-up allow yourself and your partner to do just that—warm up the body to get the parts moving. Expect awkward feelings and mistakes. You may want to stop often to re-stretch various body parts that may be feeling some strain, shake out feelings of tension, get another drink of water, shed a jacket, and take some deep breaths to relax. Sometimes just swaying together in dance position can relax you. Figure out what works for you. Keep verbal comments to a minimum during this stage.

As you begin to move into the main body of the lesson or practice session, be aware that you are moving into territory in which more interpersonal problems may surface. After all, if everything is going really well in one dance or one part of a dance, you and your partner are likely to agree to move on to an area that needs more work. This is a perfectly logical and reasonable way to use time in a lesson or practice session, but at the same time, by focusing on "problem" areas, or areas which need more work, we unintentionally invite trouble!

Think about this from the perspective of psychological defenses. Within our inner self, each of us is set up to defend ourselves in order to maintain our self-esteem. Thus, our natural tendency is to say, in our heart of hearts, "If I am sincerely trying and something goes wrong despite my best efforts, it is probably not my fault."

The next step in this chain of logic is to imagine, "If it is not my fault, then the fault must lie elsewhere." And be warned, the speed of this reaction can startle you!

Strive for Open-Mindedness

There are many possible candidates for where the fault may lie outside of the self. If you have spent much time around dancers, you are already quite familiar with the long list of "What-is-wrong-with-my-dancing-because-it-certainly-isn't-me" culprits:

- The floor is too fast/too slow.
- There is a rhinestone on the bottom of my shoe.
- My feet/knees hurt.
- I didn't have lunch.
- The ballroom is too hot/cold.
- Another couple got in our way.

But the candidate who is always available to blame for problems is your partner. Unless you are practicing alone, your partner is always there, and truth be told, your partner is never perfect. The eternal, reliable truth that our partners are not perfect makes it all too easy to ignore the equal truth that we are not perfect, either. Each of us must fight the desire to blame our partner when things are not going well in the dancing.

> He who cannot dance blames the floor.
>
> *Hindu Proverb*

Our private, inner thoughts, of course, are free. We can think whatever we want. (And we all have moments when our thoughts about our partners are dark and evil.) But what we show externally will make a huge difference in whether we are able to create and maintain a dance partnership that will work over time. At times when things are not going well in the dancing, don't say those mean things you are thinking! Take a deep breath, then make a special effort to show respect by speaking nicely to your partner and refraining from placing blame.

> ## Blame is the enemy of partnership!
> *Art and Betty Seagull*

Aside from the great benefit that will accrue to the partner relationship because of your forbearance, refraining from blaming your partner (*especially when you most want to*) has another great benefit. It actually helps you keep an open mind.

To change what you do with your body, you must be willing to change what you think. Therefore, to improve your dancing, you must be willing to accept new ideas about what is happening as you and your partner move your bodies through space to create the dance.

When you openly blame your partner you begin to set your mind toward the idea that you do not have to change anything in yourself. Yet in dancing, just as in life, there is no such thing as a one-sided relationship problem. If something is going wrong in partnered dancing, *each* person must change something.

> ## Let us be a little humble; let us think that the truth may not perhaps be entirely with us.
> *Jawaharlal Nehru*

It is amazing how hard this is to believe, no matter how many times it is demonstrated. We have to keep re-learning it. One of the first times we learned this made a big impression. We were studying the waltz, in which a natural turn (a turn to the right) is a basic figure. We had tried practicing it on our own, yet we couldn't seem to get as much turn in the figure as we wanted. We attempted various approaches to try to make it work, then gave up and took the problem to our next dance lesson. Our teacher watched us try, and then said, "Of course you can't get around. Betty's head position is preventing you from making the turn."

The idea that the lady's head position affects the quality of the turn was entirely new to us. As bronze level social dancers, we could not possibly have come up with such a notion. Until then we only knew how to make changes involving footwork or frame (upper body position).

At that moment we were both struck by how futile it would have been for us to have had a spat about that particular problem during our practice, as neither of us had a hypothesis that was anywhere near what the professional could tell us was actually the crucial change needed. In other words, although during our practice we both felt we were right, we were actually both off the mark.

Of course, many other things affect the quality of movement in a natural turn, and we will never run out of things to work on to improve those turns until we are too old to move, but that is something we didn't find out until later...

Use the Rule of Three

So how did we avoid that dance spat? We avoided it by applying the **Rule of Three**. Early in our attempts to learn to dance, we discovered that it is easy to get into a spat when you are practicing dancing. Each person thinks they know what they are supposed to do and tries to convince the other. If that works, fine. But what if it doesn't work? As a married couple, we had a relationship to preserve that was more important to us than dancing, so we developed the **Rule of Three: Try a move three different ways and if you still can't make it work, write it down and take it to the next lesson.**

The **Rule of Three** gives partners the opportunity to try it "my" way, "your" way, and one other way that we think might work. If all three of these fail, it is quite likely that there is a missing piece somewhere. Most often there is one more thing that your teacher showed you but didn't emphasize, or you just didn't get. Or, perhaps, one or both of you have misinterpreted something.

Translating language into body movements is complex. How much time have you spent in lessons trying to understand what simple words mean within a dance context? For example, what does it mean to go "forward?" Does it mean "toward my partner," "down the line of dance," or something else?

Applying the **Rule of Three** will save you endless time and aggravation during practice sessions, while preserving both self-respect and a respectful partner relationship. (More about handling dance spats in Chapter 6.)

So, having begun the lesson or practice session on a positive note, and having handled challenges during the practice or lesson with respectful behavior, it should then be natural and easy to conclude by thanking your partner at the end of each practice session or lesson.

> "Please" and "thank you" are the "basics" of respect.
>
> **Art and Betty Seagull**

Respect Your Teacher

In addition to showing respect for yourself and your partner, the third person you must respect is the person teaching you. As in choosing a partner, begin by choosing as a teacher or coach someone whose knowledge and skill you respect. If you think you know more than they do about dancing, you should not be paying them for a lesson. If you think you know less, then behave accordingly.

Arrive on time. Greet your teacher cheerfully upon arrival. Dress appropriately. Be ready to learn. Pay attention. Listen to instructions and try to follow them. Ask for help without implying that the teacher is at fault for having taught you inadequately. And always thank your teacher at the end of the lesson.

> Effective teaching may be the hardest job there is.
>
> *William Glasser*

Yes, learning to dance is challenging, but have a little empathy for your teacher. Effective teaching of ballroom dancing may be the hardest kind of teaching of all! A good dance teacher must combine high-level dance skills with the interpersonal skills of a good nursery-school teacher: enthusiasm, kindness, patience, and the calm firmness to deal with meltdowns and tantrums. It's not easy.

Ask Questions Respectfully

Good teachers and coaches put a lot of thought and energy into trying to find the best ways of conveying their wealth of information and depth of understanding to the dancer. Language is an important tool for conveying this information, but it can also become a barrier because dancing is a physical skill. Furthermore, different dancers benefit from different teaching styles, and different points need to be worked on at various stages in the development of the dancer. So it is not at all unusual to be confused, and to feel that you are being taught things that are incompatible and contradictory.

When this occurs, you *do* need to ask a clarifying question. Out of your frustration and desire to learn, your question may easily come across as disrespectful toward the teacher or coach. If that person feels insulted, you will not get the most from your lesson. Therefore, the more frustrated you feel, the more careful you should be about how to phrase your question.

For example, saying, "What! How can you say that when last week you said the opposite?" comes across as a challenge to the teacher's knowledge or skill. It may, in fact, accurately reflect your internal feeling which might be something like, "You are trying to drive me crazy!" But conveying this will not improve your progress in learning to dance or your relationship with your coach. Try saying, instead, something like, "I feel confused. I seem to remember that you told me X last week, and now Y sounds like it is the opposite. There must be something I'm not understanding. Can you help me with this?"

This type of phrasing conveys your confusion but invites your coach to help you sort it out. A direct challenge, "That's not what the champion said at the seminar last week," shifts the focus away from the dancing and on to who is "right." A statement that appears as a direct challenge to the coach's skill or authority tends to result in a response to defend that position. Yes, teachers and coaches are people, too, and they have psychological defenses just like everyone else. Arguing with them will not be the best way to use those precious and expensive minutes in your lesson.

We will have more to say in Chapter 8 about how to use your lessons most effectively. For now, just try to pretend your dance teacher is not trying to drive you crazy and treat him or her with respect.

Respect Other Dancers

Show respect for other dancers. If you are in a class, everyone is there to learn. Kidding is often part of the fun but be aware that dancing makes people feel vulnerable and feelings are easily hurt. *Do not* comment unfavorably on other people's dancing. (At least, not to their face. If you want to be privately catty with your spouse on the way home, well, that's one of the perks of marriage...). What if you're not married? In that case, forbear. Anything you have said can and will be used against you if the relationship breaks up. If you must gossip, then do it with a dear friend in another state who doesn't know any of the people involved. Otherwise, it's just too risky. Gossip has a way of coming back and biting you in the end.

If the teacher has you switch partners, try your best to do your part, and then thank your temporary partner at the end of the dance, whether things have gone well or not. Try to find something true to say to compliment your temporary partner, such as, "You have a good feeling for the music," Or, "I love your positive attitude!" These things are often accurate, even if you haven't executed the new dance step well together.

Practice Good Manners

> Along with learning the ballroom steps, Miss Manners would like to request that neo-dancers practice ballroom manners.
>
> **Judith Martin**

Not only do etiquette rules for ballroom dancing help regulate the activity, but behaving with good manners is also one of the clearest ways to show respect for self and others. Since people function best in social settings when they have some idea of what is expected of them, we present below ten basic rules of etiquette for social ballroom dancing. As we expect everyone to behave well while they are in the ballroom, we will refer to dancers as ladies and gentlemen.*

Etiquette for Social Ballroom Dancing

1. Although gentlemen traditionally ask ladies to dance, the reverse is increasingly common and acceptable. In more and more places nowadays, same gender couples may dance. Regardless of who asks whom, this invitation should be tendered graciously, for example, "May I have this dance?" or, "Would you like to waltz?
"When you invite someone to dance, look your prospective partner in the eye, smile, and speak clearly enough that she can hear.

2. The lady should respond with eye contact, a smile and an equally gracious word of thanks, for example, "Thank you, I'd love to."

---

* Teachers: Feel free to make copies of the dance etiquette rules below and hand them out to your students, as long as you credit the source.

BALLROOM DANCING IS NOT FOR SISSIES

In the rare instance that the lady refuses the offer, it must be on the grounds that she does not know how to do the dance or is "sitting this one out" (for example, is tired, is going to the powder room, getting water, and so on). It is never acceptable to refuse the offer of a dance with one partner only to accept an offer from another, presumably more attractive, partner for the same dance. (This rule assumes that all present are ladies and gentlemen, and that no one present would behave in such a way that their offensive behavior would constitute reasonable grounds for refusal. Of course, you may certainly refuse to dance with someone who is acting outside of the rules of acceptable behavior, for example, someone who is drunk.)

3. When moving into dance position, the gentleman offers his left hand and right arm as the "frame;" the lady determines the placement of her body within this frame.

4. Dancers move in a counterclockwise direction around the perimeter of the dance floor. This is commonly referred to as, "the line of dance."

5. Couples doing spot dances (such as swing or rumba) should move into the middle of the floor so that they do not obstruct the flow of traffic along the line of dance. For the same reason, those who wish to stop and chat should move off the dance floor entirely.

6. The gentleman determines what dance will be danced to the music being played and the direction and timing of movement. This is the essence of the "lead." The lady strives to "follow" by matching the gentleman's timing and movement. (We discuss issues involved in leading and following in more depth in Chapter 4.)

7. As far as possible, the gentleman should lead only those patterns that he believes the lady can follow. If he does not know his partner's dance level, he should err on the side of caution by leading more basic patterns, increasing the complexity of the patterns he leads only if his partner seems comfortable.

8. If errors are made, it is polite to appear not to notice them. If noticing them is unavoidable, both partners should take responsibility for them, regardless of whether they really think they are at fault. (Obviously, this would be different during a lesson, when the teacher will naturally work on correcting errors.)

In the unfortunate event of a "crash" between dance couples, each couple should ask if the other is hurt and provide any assistance needed. Everyone should apologize and, unlike a car crash, everyone should strive to take responsibility and minimize the level of pain, injury, or embarrassment that has occurred.

9. When dancing socially with a partner whose ability level you believe to be above yours, avoid apologizing profusely before, during, or after the dance. Denigrating oneself is never charming, and is likely to make the partner uncomfortable. One can compliment the lovely dancing of one's partner without making self-derogatory remarks.

10. When the music stops, the gentleman should escort the lady to her seat, smile and thank her for the dance. Likewise, she should smile and thank him.

Respect the Activity

Would you expect to learn to play tennis in one easy lesson? No? How about golf? Well, maybe ice hockey—surely that's easy—just slap on some skates and go. Sounds ridiculous, doesn't it? We recognize that learning to play a sport, whether a team or individual sport, takes time and practice. Why would we think learning to dance is any different?

Yet consider this actual class description taken from a community education bulletin: "Holiday parties are the perfect time to shine! Join us for this one time class to learn steps in the Fox Trot (for traditional dancing), Tango (for the popular Latin beat), and the Swing to impress them all. Then you can have a great time with any music they play."

This is an ad for a 90-minute class. With the outlandish promise it makes, any couple who attends is guaranteed only one outcome—by the time this class is over, they will feel hopelessly dumb and be totally discouraged when they don't learn the fox trot, tango, and swing in an hour and a half.

Another example—when we are out dancing socially we are often complimented by couples we don't know. The compliments sound something like this.

Woman: "We just love your dancing! It was so much fun to watch you!"

Man: "Do you take lessons?"

Us: "Yes."

Man to woman (in a knowing tone), "See, I told you so!"

Maybe this is a straightforward compliment. But there are times when the "do-you-take-lessons" question feels like an unspoken implication that if we took lessons we somehow cheated. Only if we "naturally" danced beautifully did we really deserve credit for the compliment. If that's what people are thinking, it's a weird idea.

So have some respect for this activity. Dancing with a partner is a complex skill that takes time, patience, and practice to learn, especially if you want to do it well. The "anyone can do it" or "should be able to do it" attitude is simply nonsense. "Anyone can do it with training and practice" is a more truthful and respectful idea.

> So you can't dance? Not at all? Not even one step? . . .How can you say that you've taken any trouble to live when you won't even dance?
>
> *Hermann Hesse*

Review of Bronze Level Respect: Stand Up and Smile!

Respect yourself

* Exercise: Practicing Posture and Self-Respect
* Use positive self-talk
* Be kind to yourself

Respect your partner

* Exercise: Practicing Respect for Your Partner
* Warm-Up
* Strive for open-mindedness
* Use the Rule of Three

Respect your teacher

* Ask questions respectfully

Respect other dancers

* Practice good manners

Respect the activity

Chapter 3

BRONZE LEVEL RESPONSIBILITY: STAY OVER YOUR OWN FEET AND ON YOUR OWN SIDE

Couples Share a Brain

The comedienne, Roseanne, used to joke, "Men think the womb is a homing device. 'Honey, where are my socks? Where are my slippers?'" This familiar scenario always got a big laugh of recognition from her audiences.

> "I must do something," always solves more problems than, "Something must be done."
>
> *Anonymous*

But it isn't just men who depend on women. It works both ways. Women often depend on their husbands to keep track of when the car needs an oil change, or whether the gas in the lawnmower is low. This is what couples commonly do. Psychologists call it "cognitive off-loading." They decrease the amount of information they have to keep in their brains by dividing tasks between members of the couple. Not only do they divide actually performing the tasks, they also divide responsibility for thinking about the tasks. This is a useful strategy, since each person then has fewer details to keep track of and can depend on their spouse for the rest of them.

When Sharing a Brain Works

Decreasing the amount of stuff you have to think about by delegating responsibility for certain areas to the other member of the couple can be a successful strategy if the following conditions are met:

- The members of the couple *agree on who is responsible for what.* Example: "If you'll do the dishes, I'll vacuum the living room."
- The division of labor *feels fair* to both people. Example: "I would much rather wash than dry and you like to dry, so I'll wash the dishes and you dry them, and we'll both be happy."
- The person who is *not* doing the task shows *a lot of appreciation* to the person who is doing it, thanking and encouraging them. Example: "Thank you so much for cleaning the toilets! I really appreciate that you noticed they needed cleaning, and just took care of it! Great job!"
- The person who is not doing the task *refrains from criticizing* the frequency, quality, or method chosen by the person doing it. Example: In the toilet-cleaning example above, the spouse does *not* say, "I can't believe you let the toilets get so filthy before you cleaned them." (In the face of such negativity, how eager do you think the person would be to do this job again?)
- Each member of the couple *does the jobs they agreed to do and refrains from doing the other person's job.* Example: The non-toilet-cleaning spouse does not take over this job unless the couple negotiates a new agreement.
- The couple has skills for renegotiating as needed. Example: "Now that we have a baby, we need to rethink our division of labor because a lot of new tasks have been added to our life!"

When all six aspects of task sharing and delegation of responsibility are observed according to the above principles, life is good. Things that need to be done get done, and everyone feels secure and appreciated.

When Sharing a Brain is a Problem

Sharing a brain by using cognitive off-loading to split up responsibility for the work a couple needs to do sounds like a great idea—an efficient use of resources. But lack of success in negotiating and carrying out the division of family labor is one of the most common types of problems we see in our psychological work with couples who have marital problems. Why? Simply put, taking responsibility for ourselves and not taking responsibility for the other person are two of the biggest challenges in any relationship. (Failure to negotiate a successful agreement for division of labor in the first place usually stems from unexamined differences in values between members of the couple. But in dancing, the roles are assigned, so we will not take up that problem in the present discussion.)

Lack of success in carrying out the division of labor tends to fall into three common patterns:

1. Criticizing the other person because they are doing the task "wrong" (Example: "Don't fold the towels across first, fold them down first, then across.").

2. Trying to be helpful because the other person's method seems inefficient or ineffective (Example: "If you would soak that pot overnight, it would be a lot easier to scrub.").

3. Simply taking over a task the other person had agreed to do ("I went ahead and balanced the checkbook because letting it go unbalanced for a week was driving me crazy!").

The problem with even the well-meant, "helpful" criticism of the first two patterns is that people don't like being criticized. Often, the recipient of the criticism is even angrier if the critic is correct! People tend to feel personally attacked, and respond by defending their position. The argument that follows often ends with, "If you don't like the way I do it, do it yourself!"

Over time, the more perfectionist, critical, or efficient spouse often takes over more and more of the tasks, and then complains about not getting enough help. It is common for women to "overfunction" in this way, to the point where family roles deteriorate into a "critical mother/naughty boy" relationship, instead of a husband/wife partnership. This same dynamic is easily reproduced in the dance lesson.

The flip side of these patterns is for a partner to shirk his or her agreed-upon responsibilities, either deliberately (passive-aggressively) or because he or she is disorganized, overwhelmed by too many responsibilities, or is incompetent at performing the tasks they agreed upon. Many couple fights occur because one member of the couple believes that the other one is deliberately shirking a responsibility, when, in truth, the spouse's failure stems from poor organization or distraction by other stresses.

In a dance partnership it is rare for a member of the couple to actively shirk responsibility for performing their role. If people don't want to dance, they simply quit. It is, after all, an optional activity. As for incompetence, that feeling is familiar to dancers! But it is our teacher's job to help us with that, not our partner's.

The third pattern, simply taking over the other person's role, happens a lot, especially in beginning dance partnerships. "Stay over your own feet and on your own side" means, "Take responsibility for doing your part and don't interfere with me when I'm trying to do my part!"

In dancing, taking over the partner's role often occurs because of confusion about how to actually execute one's role properly. Confusion about what it means to "lead" and "follow" is especially common. We will go into more detail about this aspect of role confusion in Chapter 4. Right now, let's take a look at what happens when one dance partner gives "helpful criticism" to the other.

Trying to Share a Brain While Dancing

Tom and Tanya are warming up at the beginning of their fourth dance lesson. "You are supposed to start with your left foot," says Tanya, "and you're not dancing in time to the music."

"OK," says Tom, and tries again. This time he begins with his left foot and Tanya says, "You are doing the pattern wrong. It should be forward, side, together, but you aren't bringing your feet together like the teacher said."

Tom replies, "I told you I had two left feet. You were the one who wanted to take dance lessons!" This couple is on the way to becoming dance school drop-outs.

As this example illustrates, dancing brings out the dynamics of responsibility in relationships very quickly because partnered dancing expresses the relationship physically, so that roles and responsibilities are easily seen and clearly experienced. If Tom and Tanya decide to persevere instead of dropping out, dancing will provide them with an arena in which they can work on sharpening their relationship skills in sharing and delegating tasks.

Have you ever been in a work situation in which a supervisor delegated a job to you, and then did the job him/herself? Can you recall how infuriating this was? You probably wanted to say something like, "Don't ask me to do something, and then do it yourself! It wastes my time, and is disrespectful to me. It indicates that you either don't trust me, or you think I'm incompetent!"

Tom may be having those thoughts, and the feelings that go with them, when Tanya "helpfully" criticizes him. She needs to back off and let Tom figure this out for himself, instead of trying to be in charge of his dancing as well as hers. Although her intention is to be helpful, if she takes over keeping track of the details he is supposed to be paying attention to, she is actually hindering his learning. In effect, she is trying to dance both parts when, in fact, she is only responsible for dancing her own part.

So what can she focus on while she is waiting for Tom to figure out what he is doing? She can practice taking responsibility for herself.

Practicing Individual Responsibility

A fascinating thing about the dance partnership is that harmonious partnered movement is created from separateness. Each person can dance *only* their own part. The more skilled each individual is at dancing his or her own part, the better the couple will be. "But," we can hear you objecting, "I can't dance my best if my partner isn't dancing correctly!"

> Take your life in your own hands, and what happens? A terrible thing: no one to blame.
>
> *Erica Jong*

There is some truth to this. We all have a tendency to dance "up" to a higher level if we are dancing with a more proficient partner. A more skilled partner has a greater ability to compensate and cover for our errors, so that we feel we are dancing better. And a more skilled partner is less likely to make overt errors that make it impossible for us to dance our part. This is what happens when you dance with the teacher. And this is one reason why pro-am dancing (a professional dancing with an amateur) is so popular. But even if you dance with a teacher, you still have to take responsibility for dancing your own part.

So what can you do to practice responsibility? To begin with, practice coming to the lesson a little ahead of time so you have a chance to prepare yourself. Different people require different preparation to make the transition from whatever they have been doing and thinking to focusing on dancing.

Take responsibility for learning what *you* need to do to prepare. Perhaps you need to hang up your coat and change your shoes. Possibly you need to use the restroom and change into a practice outfit. It is always a good idea to stretch before any exercise. Dancing is no exception.

Maybe you want to socialize with the other dancers before you begin. Whatever it is that *you* need to do, make time for it in your schedule.

> Action springs not from thought, but from a readiness for responsibility.
> **Dietrich Bonhoeffer**

Dress in clothing that will allow you to move comfortably. Pants or skirts that are too tight may limit your stride. Ballroom dance shoes are, of course, best for dancing, but if you haven't yet bought your first pair of ballroom shoes, wear street shoes with soles that are flexible. Rigid soles will prevent you from flexing your foot. And make sure the soles of your shoes are clean. No one appreciates mud, sand, and dirt tracked onto the dance floor. Dirty shoes are more than an annoyance; they can actually create a hazard for you and for other dancers.

Example: Responsibility for Self (Bronze Level)

A woman often arrived late for her dance class. When she got there, she would complain loudly about having had to wait for a train, blaming the railway for the slow train and the city for not building an underpass. This disrupted the lesson for other people. Then she would need additional instruction, having missed the introduction. One day her teacher said to her:

"Can you take responsibility for getting here on time?"

"Well, I can't do anything about the train schedule!" she retorted.

"That is true," said the teacher, "I wonder how you can work with what is within your control."

After the woman got over her anger, she thought about what her teacher had said. Suddenly, she realized she could start out earlier in order to drive across the tracks before the train got there, or take a different route. After that she took responsibility for what she *could* control.

Take responsibility for your attitude and behavior during the lesson. Mental preparation includes being open to new learning. And need we say that you cannot learn anything if you are under the influence of substances? No drugs or alcohol before the lesson.

The best mind-altering drug is truth.

Lily Tomlin

Whether you are learning a new pattern or reviewing one you already understand, you can always work on your posture. Try to be aware of starting with good posture, and maintain it as well as you can. When you notice yourself drooping, pick up your posture again. Your posture is your responsibility. You will be amazed at how much you can strengthen and tone the muscles in your torso just from the isometric exercise of working on your posture.

Similarly, your balance is your responsibility. Try to be aware of keeping your own weight over your own feet. Never lean on your partner. Never allow your partner to pull you off your balance. The more you are grounded and centered within yourself, the more difficult it will be for a partner to disturb your balance. Like every aspect of dancing, this will take time to develop, but it is never too soon to begin.

When it's your turn to move, go ahead and move, rather than waiting for your partner to move you. If you step on each other in the process, this will be useful feedback about your position (you are not staying on your own side of the couple's center) or timing (you are not matching your partner).

Remember that **Respect** is the first of the **3 Rs**. If things don't go well, take responsibility for being respectful in your response. Avoid blaming your partner, the teacher, or the couple next to you.

> The willingness to accept responsibility for one's own life is the source from which self-respect springs.
>
> *Joan Didion*

Respect yourself. Give sincere apologies for mistakes, but do it without denigrating yourself. Say, "Oh, I'm sorry, I started on the wrong foot," not, "Oh, what a hopeless klutz I am!"

Allow the teacher to teach. Be quiet and pay attention when the teacher is talking. Watch what is being demonstrated and try to imitate it. Wait for the instructor to finish before asking a question. You may find that s/he is coming to the point you wanted to ask about. Ask questions respectfully, and be aware that others have needs, too. Do not monopolize the class. If you need more of the instructor's time than you can get in a group class, you may find it helpful to schedule some time for private lessons to supplement your learning.

Responsibility Checklist for Dance Lessons (Bronze Level)

As a student of dance it is your responsibility to:

- Be on time.
- Dress appropriately.
- Be mentally and physically prepared to learn.
- Be polite and respectful.
- Cultivate good posture.
- Maintain your own balance.
- Move yourself.
- Stay on your own side.
- Refrain from criticizing others.
- Allow the teacher to teach.

Do not try to teach your partner or anyone else. Be patient and, to put it bluntly, "mind your own business." If another student asks you how to do a pattern, refer them to the teacher, even if you think you know the answer. This might sound rude, but it is really not. In your attempt to be helpful you may just end up confusing them more.

This takes us to the other half of the skill of taking responsibility in a partnership. One half is taking responsibility for yourself. The other half is *refraining* from taking responsibility for your partner. This is much more difficult than it sounds. People want to be helpful, especially if they are in a social relationship with their partner. Or, in a more troubled relationship, they want to be right. Neither is actually helpful.

Practicing Separateness

In dancing we speak of "staying on our own side." In a basic dance position, we are slightly offset to the left as we face our partner. This prevents us from stepping on each other's feet, allowing the moving leg to swing between the partner's legs. Just as we have to stay on our own side to allow our partner to move and avoid stepping on each other's feet physically, we have to stay on our own side to allow our partner to move psychologically.

Let the teacher do the teaching, and don't try to help. The simple fact is that *most of our efforts to help our partner are not helpful because our partner is having a different experience.* This is so difficult to believe that we ask you to take this on faith for now. And the corollary is the most difficult of all to believe: *This is true even if what you are telling your partner is correct.*

Remember cognitive off-loading? When it works well, it works not just because jobs are delegated. It works because *the mental work of keeping track of tasks is divided.* This works in dancing, too.

Take responsibility *only* for yourself. Stay on your own side and be patient and empathic with your partner. Your partner is having a different experience. Allow your partner the physical and psychological space to experience and grow.

Tom and Tanya Warm Up Responsibly

So what would it look like if Tom and Tanya took this advice? Remember them from earlier in this chapter? If both of them were trying to take responsibility *only* for themselves, their warm-up might go something like this: Tom starts with the wrong foot.

Tanya says, smiling, "Gosh! I guess we were on different feet! Let's try again." Now Tom uses the other foot and dances off time. Tanya says nothing. They stumble a little as they try to make the pattern work. Tom says, "I'm sorry, I guess I stepped on you." Tanya replies, "It's OK, you didn't mean to." Tanya takes a deep breath and tries to practice individual posture and smiling. Tom says, "I can't remember how this goes. Do you remember how to do it?" Tanya: "Hmm, I'm not sure. Maybe we should ask the teacher."

How to be Helpful

The two best ways to be helpful to your partner are: (1) do your own part as well as you can, and (2) say positive and encouraging things to your partner. If you can only do one of these, the first is the more important. Doing your own part well is the greatest contribution you can make to the partnership. The second is important not only because we all need a pat on the back when we are trying to learn something new, but because it gives you something to do instead of helping or criticizing.

Our brains don't process negative information very well. That is why every program designed to help people stop smoking or overeating provides ideas for behaviors to do *in place of* the behavior they are trying to decrease. Just saying, "Don't smoke," isn't very helpful. It works better to offer a series of alternatives to do in those situations in which people habitually smoke. Many people chew gum, for example, when they are trying to stop smoking. It gives them something to do instead.

In the same way, instead of criticizing or coaching your partner, pay attention to things your partner is doing well and improvements he or she is making. Focus on the positive and look for things about which you can give your partner a sincere compliment. Then practice giving and receiving compliments.

Exercise: Giving and Receiving a Compliment

Sit or stand facing your partner. Looking into your partner's eyes, give a sincere compliment, phrased as an "I-message." (More about "I-messages" in Chapter 6.) The content may be about anything. It does not have to be about dancing. It must be honest.

Example: "I really appreciate how hard you are trying. I admire your courage and willingness to keep at this."

The person receiving the compliment should smile and say, "Thank you."

Now reverse roles of giver and recipient, and repeat.

Note how you feel. Is it difficult to give a sincere compliment? Is it difficult to receive a compliment with grace? If so, what might be the obstacles for you?

Practice this compliment exercise before and after every dance lesson. Does it get easier with time? How does it feel within the partnership?

Taking responsibility for giving and receiving compliments will enhance your skill in all of your relationships. The more you practice honestly giving and receiving positive feedback, the better you, and everyone around you, will feel.

When you blame others, you give up your power to change.

Anonymous

So "stay over your own feet" (take responsibility for yourself) and "stay on your own side" (allow your partner to experience and execute what is his/her responsibility). And then something unexpected may happen.

Enjoying Separateness

An unforeseen bonus of practicing separateness is that after awhile you will begin to enjoy it! Instead of having to take responsibility for two people, you only have to take responsibility for yourself. This is actually a relief.

The only behavior you can directly change is your own. Practicing separateness while dancing will spill over into your non-dancing relationships in positive ways. Instead of thinking, "How can I get this person to change?" when there is a problem, you will develop the habit of thinking, "What can I do to improve this situation?"

If you are someone who has tended to over-function in relationships, doing more than your half, you will learn to back off and let the other person step up and struggle with fulfilling their responsibility. And if you are someone who has tended to let others do more than half the work, you will be more aware of the need to do your part. Finding ways to have a more equitable division of responsibility in all your relationships will bring you into balance in life, as well as in dancing.

> Sing and dance together and be joyous, but let each one of you be alone
>
> Even as the strings of a lute are alone though they quiver with the same music...
>
> And stand together yet not too near together
>
> For the pillars of the temple stand apart
>
> And the oak tree and the cypress grow not in each others shadow
>
> *Kahlil Gibran*

Review of Bronze Level Responsibility: Stay over Your Own Feet and on Your Own Side

Couples divide responsibility by sharing a brain
* This works when:
    * Partners agree on division of responsibility.
    * Division of responsibility feels fair to both.
    * Partners show appreciation.
    * Partners refrain from criticism.
    * Each person does their job and only their job.
    * Partners renegotiate as needed.
* Common problems in life, and in dancing:
    * Criticizing
    * Being overly helpful
    * Taking over

Practice individual responsibility (stay over your own feet)
* Review responsibility checklist

Practice separateness (stay on your own side)
* Do your own part.
* Encourage your partner. (Exercise: Giving and Receiving a Compliment)
* Refrain from criticizing or helping
* Let the teacher teach.
* Allow your partner to have his/her own experience.

Chapter 4

BRONZE LEVEL RESPONSIVENESS: LEADING AND FOLLOWING

"Who's in Charge?"

Like a lot of women, Susan had wanted to take dance lessons for years, but, like a lot of men, her husband, Sam, resisted. "I'm a klutz," he said. "I'd rather watch TV."

Finally, Susan saw her opportunity—a local dance studio was advertising a Valentine's Day special. Susan bought a package of dance lessons as a gift for Sam. What could he do? He had to go. And, to everyone's surprise, after the first lesson, Sam was hooked. It hadn't been so bad, after all. He had actually enjoyed it! But Susan had changed her mind. "I don't want a man telling me what to do." They never went back.

The Gender Role Tradition

Back in the days when the waltz, the fox trot, and the rumba were invented, assigning tasks by gender was a social practice which was a given in all areas of life. Men shoveled the walk, women cooked dinner. In those days it was taken for granted that the man should "lead" and the woman should "follow."

> Dancing's just a conversation between two people. Talk to me.
> *Hope Floats*

In those days, a respectable woman would not have asked a man on a date, and would not have asked a man to dance at a social function. And same-sex partnerships were deep, deep in the closet. Now all of that has changed.

Nowadays, in the world of work, women have become quite aware of the importance of seizing opportunities to exert leadership if they are interested in being promoted. Modern women value being strong and assertive. And many of these women are put off by the idea that partnered dancing assigns the role of "follower" to them. Following someone else's lead in the world of work can be a bad strategy that will lead to a dead-end job—or a layoff. So being asked to "follow" in dancing rubs many women the wrong way. To make matters even worse, teachers who have not kept up to date with the most current teaching methods are, unfortunately, still teaching men to "lead" by exerting pressure on the woman's upper body with their hands and arms. This style of leading is very uncomfortable for the woman. She feels like she is being pushed around—because she is! And she doesn't like it.

Men typically have more upper body strength than women, so if they are taught to "lead" using the outdated push-and-pull system, they are likely to use much more force than they realize. To the woman, this easily feels like a microcosm of abuse. A natural and healthy response to feeling like you are being pushed is to resist. So the woman resists, and often feels angry in the process. Then the man, who realizes that his partner is not "following," tries even harder to "lead" by exerting more force. The woman feels even more abused, and resists more. Nothing good can come from such a system.

Rethinking "Lead and Follow"

To a man, the idea that "the man gets to lead" seems right, or, at best, seems like no big deal, but this is an important barrier to partnered dancing for many women. Furthermore, the "brute strength" method of leading simply does not work. When we were first taught by this method, we found that we *both* came home from an evening of dancing with pain in our arms, shoulders, and back, as we tried to deal with the forces of pushing and pulling.

The current system of training replaces the upper-body "brute" lead with a "move yourself" system. In this system, the man moves *his own* body without exerting force on the woman, and the woman *moves herself* to fill the space he creates for her. The "lead" is still communicated partly through the man's "frame," (torso-shoulder-arm complex), which has tone but is flexible, rather than rigid. The woman's frame is correspondingly toned and she is attuned to shifts in the man's body as he shapes and moves himself. The more important part of the lead, however, is communicated by the lower body. For example, when the man bends his knee or settles his hip in a compression, the woman learns to feel that and understands the message it sends, "Get ready, we are about to move!" She can then be prepared to *respond* by moving herself.

Learning this method of leading and following may sound pretty challenging. Well, yes, it is. It takes time and patience— and this may be a reason why the old "brute" method is still being taught. That method can provide a "quick fix," but it is like repairing your broken muffler with chewing gum and duct tape. The "fix" won't last long and it isn't safe!

> Dancing is wonderful training for girls; it's the first way you learn to guess what a man is going to do before he does it.
>
> *Christopher Morley*

If you are just learning to dance, the descriptions of "lead and follow" in the rest of this chapter may feel too complicated. That is OK. Beginning dancers first need to learn some patterns.

But we want to talk about "lead and follow" issues up front because they can present so many relationship problems for couples at all levels of skill. We believe that it is helpful for you to hear a number of different ways to think about leading and following. And we ask you to take on faith that the way "leading and following" is typically presented in beginning classes is just a place to start—it's not the way things will always be. If you stay with your dancing, you and your partner will gradually get hooked on the fun and the challenge of learning to attune yourselves to each other, so that, over time, you will learn to pass the "lead" back and forth between you.

The Rules of the Game

"Getting away from the 'brute strength' method of leading sounds like a great idea," you may be thinking, "but doesn't it still leave the man in charge? What about that?"

Well, yes and no. Think for a moment about what the man's "lead" consists of. It no longer means that only the man may ask the woman to dance. Plenty of women now ask men to dance. And same-sex dance partnerships are increasingly common, even among straight people, because numbers of men and women at a dance event are not always even. But when a same-gender couple dances, they have to decide who is dancing which part, and who gets to pick the timing and direction of movement. That is the essence of the "lead." The "leader" gets to choose what dance to dance (for example, fox trot or swing, which may sometimes be danced to the same music), where to orient the couple on the dance floor, and when to begin dancing. (And, ladies, if he chooses to dance a rumba to a cha cha... try not to grind your teeth too loudly, smile and practice your posture!)

Professional dancers, of course, know how to dance both parts, so they have the freedom to change who is dancing which part if they want. We saw a wonderful show where this was beautifully demonstrated. World 10-Dance Champions, Alain Doucet and Anik Jolicoeur, together with Canadian Latin Champions, Jean-Marc Genereux and France Mousseau, did a show in which all possible combinations of dancers danced together at different times in the routine—Alain and Anik danced not only with each other, but Anik with Jean-Marc, France with Alain, the two women together, the two men together, and at times the women also danced the men's part while the men danced the women's part. It was fantastic to see how beautifully they moved through all the various combinations. But this requires a very high level of skill.

Most of us have enough to keep track of just to dance our own part, especially when we are first learning to dance. So it is most useful to think about "lead and follow" not in terms of "who is in charge" but as a convenience that helps us begin each dance without having to negotiate who is doing what. It is simply a "rule of the game," like dealing a certain number of cards to each player at the beginning of a card game.

But He Gets to Pick the Patterns!

Yes, it's true. As part of the "lead" the man does have the job of selecting which patterns or figures of the dance to lead at any given time. And this can be frustrating to his partner. Many years ago we were spectators at a competition at Cobo Hall in Detroit, which has an absolutely huge dance floor. During a break in the competition, we got up to do a social waltz. The floor was extremely crowded, and Art kept leading the same figure, over and over. Betty was getting bored. "Can't we do something else?" she whispered. "No," Art replied. "I'm terrified of getting run over by all these people!"

The same thing happens when a more experienced and skilled woman is dancing with a less skilled man. She may feel disappointed that his lead does not give her the opportunity to dance some of the more complex figures she enjoys. She can't just break into a pattern on her own if he doesn't give her the opening to do it. So women must learn other ways to entertain and challenge themselves, no matter who their partner is. And there are some things she can do—which we will get to in the section on **Issues for the Lady**, below.

But first, we invite you to consider that there are several more ways to think about who is leading.

More Ways to Think about "Leading"

As you gain skill you will begin to realize that, in reality, during the course of a dance, leadership within the partnership changes from moment to moment. The teamwork in a two-person canoe is a good analogy. In canoeing, the person sitting in the stern supplies more of the power and does more of the steering, but is very dependent upon the person in the bow to read the water and call out obstacles in the stream ahead, while shifting his or her strokes to avoid them. Over time, the paddler in the stern learns to read the body movements of the partner in the bow, and can anticipate what the partner will say even before it is said—a great advantage in rapids, where it is hard to hear. Is one of those team members more important than the other? Is one of them "leading?" Each needs the other to move smoothly and safely through the water.

Supplying Power

One way to think about "leadership" in the dance partnership is to regard the person supplying the power as the leader. The partner supplying the power is the one who is "behind" the couple, facing forward. That dancer supplies power by taking a step heel-first down the floor (in a smooth or standard dance). This is known as a "heel lead." A heel step is a power step.

At the beginning of a waltz or fox trot, for example, the man will set up facing in the general direction of the line of dance (OK, he may be facing diagonal center or diagonal wall, but we won't get into that here). He bends his knee and takes a step; the woman takes a corresponding step back, responding to what she feels from him, matching the size of her stride to his. Now let us say he decides to go to promenade. This puts the woman behind the man; therefore, she supplies the power. Now she is leading, and he has to match her. In other words, each of them must be attuned to what they are feeling from their partner, and respond accordingly.

This is also true in the rhythm/Latin dances. At the beginning of the dance, the man is usually the person moving forward. He settles his hip as he prepares to dance, then communicates the "lead" through his toned frame as he releases the energy from his hip, stepping forward. The woman responds by stepping back. But just a moment later, it is her turn to go forward, putting her in the power position, as the man steps back. They must be closely attuned to each other as they rapidly pass power back and forth between them.

> A leader is best when people barely know he exists, not so good when people obey and acclaim him, worse when they despise him...But of a good leader who talks little when his work is done, his aim fulfilled, they will say, "We did it ourselves."
>
> *Lao Tzu*

First Down the Floor

Another way of thinking about leading is that the leader is the person who is "first down the floor" (for example, the lady in the start of a typical closed dance figure, where she dances backwards; the gentleman in a promenade position). Why? Because the person behind cannot run their partner over. The partner in front is the one vacating space for the partner behind to fill. This sets a limit on how much the partner behind can move.

Let's return to the waltz example. The man sets up to waltz, bends his knee, and takes his first step, but he feels that his partner does not move as much as he had in mind. Rather than knock her over, he backs off and moves less. *He adjusts his movement to hers.* So we could say she is leading. Or we could say he is *responsive* to what he feels from her.

Continuing with the example, let us say he leads a twinkle or whisk to promenade. Now the woman is in the power position, and as she tries to move down the floor, the man does not come with her with the vigor she had hoped for. She cannot drag him. So she has to back off. In reality, they take turns leading, but then each has to constantly adjust to the movements of the other. The same principle operates in the Latin/rhythm dances.

He Goes, She Goes

Another way to think about what it means for the man to "lead" is to think of it as meaning that he has the first turn. According to the rules of the game of chess, white always takes the first turn to move. In the rules of the sport of ballroom dancing, the man takes the first turn to move. He goes, and then, only a split second later, she goes. They take turns. The fact that he gets to go first doesn't mean he gets all the turns! This is a common misconception. Many men think that leadership in the dance means that the man gets to go all the time. This is far from the case. He moves in a way that opens space for his partner. This invites her to dance into it. *Then he has to wait while she does what he invited her to do.*

He goes; then she goes. Then he gets another turn. The time in which this occurs is telescoped enough that there are no big pauses to an onlooker, but a woman can certainly feel rushed or overpowered if her partner invites her to do something in the dance and then does not give her the time and the space to complete it. She *responds* to his invitation; then he must wait and feel when she is done before inviting her to do another dance figure. He must be *responsive* to her, just as she is to him.

Each partner must *respect* the other person's turn to go, and be *responsible* for their own movement when it is their turn. So, skilled turn-taking requires *respect, responsibility,* and *responsiveness,* the **3Rs of Relationship Fitness**.

She's the Picture, He's the Frame

How often have you heard this old saw, "She's the picture, he's the frame"? But it is a reasonably accurate way to summarize what goes on in ballroom dancing. When onlookers watch a ballroom couple, most will watch the lady more than the gentleman. The lady is the show. But—she cannot do it without him.

Being "the show" is the big compensation to the lady for not being able to choose the dance figures. Yes, if he doesn't lead it, she can't do it, but, with increasing skill, she will find there is more and more she really can do within the framework that is provided by the man. If you don't think so, attend a competition and watch the top professional ladies dancing with their students. The top pro ladies look like the great dancers they are even when they are dancing with beginning students who are leading basic figures, because they know how to make the most of each movement without disrespecting or overpowering their partner.

> The cock crows, but the hen delivers the goods...
>
> *Anonymous*

Have you ever been in an apartment building where the floor plan of all the apartments is the same? Yet, if you have the chance to go inside and visit, you will see that each apartment looks quite different according to the differing tastes of the residents. One decorates with massive oak furniture, heavy drapes, and dark, rich colors. Another chooses white wicker furniture, chiffon curtains, and light pastels, giving an airy look to the place. Yet another uses glass and steel furnishings, Venetian blinds, and neutral colors to create a sleek, modern look. In each case the basic structure is the same, but within that structure there is great freedom to create a look and feel that reflects the individual style of each apartment dweller.

The lady has the same freedom of choice within the structure of the dance figures being "led." The gentleman builds the basic structure and the lady has the fun of decorating it.

Keep in mind that being the "frame" doesn't mean that the man is doing nothing, or that his dancing is unimportant. Have you ever had a painting reframed and discovered what a huge difference the right frame makes in bringing out the beauty of the artwork? Or have you ever bought a picture just to get the great frame? In dancing, as in top-quality artwork, the picture and the frame complement and bring out the best in each other.

Leading Does Not Equal Forcing

So what is "leading"? If you are a man who thinks it means you get to drag your partner around the floor, or force her to do something she does not want to do, we can assure you that no one will want to dance with you. If you are a woman who thinks that "following" means being passive, you, too, will have trouble finding and keeping a dance partner. Like a modern marriage, the modern dance partnership requires active commitment, energy, and *responsiveness* from *both* partners in order to work.

> Leaders don't force people to follow—they invite them on a journey.
>
> *Charles S. Lauer*

To sum up, "leading" is *not* the same as "forcing." The gentleman leads a figure by moving and shaping *his own body*; then he waits to see if the lady accepts his invitation. He cannot force her to go, he can only invite her. The woman should strive to attune herself to what is being "led," and follow through if she is able.

If she chooses not to go, however, there is nothing the man can do about it. And if she does something he didn't have in mind, he should try to do his best to follow her! Remember, one of the things we can learn from dancing is to overcome our unrealistic perfectionism! So if something goes wrong, don't get mad, learn to laugh about it! Then talk it over later and try to figure out what happened. This mutuality of attunement within the couple is the essence of the third **R,** *responsiveness.*

Exercise: Practicing Responsiveness

Try this exercise to heighten your experience of feeling and responding to your partner, while attending to your own experience.

Preparation:

Prepare for this exercise by selecting music that does not have a recognizable dance beat—to prevent you from falling into dance patterns that you have learned. Set up your music so that you can easily push a button to begin. Plan to play the music for 2–3 minutes for each of three parts of this exercise.

Take off your shoes, to feel connected to the earth.

Each person should start with a desire for collaboration based on respect and responsibility.

Focus on your own experience, while seeking to respond to your partner.

Start the Music and Begin:

Stand facing your partner, at a comfortable distance, with your feet apart under your own shoulders.

Hold your arms in front of you, elbows bent, palms toward your partner. Connect with your partner, palm to palm. Close your eyes. Gently put weight into your partner so you can feel each other and maintain a connection.

Part 1: Allow the man to "lead" by moving as he wishes to the music. The woman should attune herself and try to follow his movements.

Stop the music after 2–3 minutes, then restart and move to Part 2.

Part 2: Allow the woman to "lead" by moving as she wishes to the music. The man should attune himself and try to follow her movements.

Stop the music after 2–3 minutes, then restart and move to Part 3.

Part 3: This time, allow the "lead" to pass back and forth between the partners. Try to attune yourself to your partner's movements. Seek a place of fluid collaboration—adjusting all the time.

Stop the music after 2–3 minutes, then discuss.

Discussion:

Try to continue a "mindful connection" as you discuss this exercise. How did this experience feel? What was it like to "lead"? What was it like to "follow"? What was it like to collaborate, with no assigned roles? What was your experience of being responsive and responded to? As you discuss, listen carefully to your partner. Ask questions only to clarify your understanding. Try to hear and understand your partner without judgment. When it is your turn to speak, notice and share how you feel. There are no "right" or "wrong" ways to have this experience. Spend as much time talking about this with your partner as you both would like.

Repeat as a warm-up exercise, a shared moment to increase awareness, or any time the partnership balance feels "off."

Issues for the Gentleman

The gentleman in the dance partnership is placed in a demanding position: he is asked to exert "leadership," even though he may feel he does not know what he is doing. This is a particular problem for the man in the beginning stages of learning to dance, but it continues to be an issue that he must confront and try to master throughout his dance career.

Multitasking

The man's problem—trying to exert leadership when he doesn't know what he is doing—is made even worse because many women learn the basic patterns faster than the men. It is not clear why this should be the case, but at least one factor that may contribute to the "man as slow learner" syndrome is that the man actually has a lot of extra material to learn in the early stages; material that the lady does not have to worry about. Dancing involves multitasking for both partners, but the gentleman has even more tasks to pay attention to than the lady does.

Scientists who have studied human multitasking have found that trying to perform even relatively easy multiple perceptual-motor tasks places heavy demands on the brain's information processing system. First the brain must encode the task stimulus, then select the appropriate response, and finally, produce the movements required to execute the response. Meanwhile, his dance partner is saying, "So why don't we start already?!"

The reason the couple hasn't started to dance is that the gentleman is thinking, "What dance is this?" and then, "What pattern should I lead?" and then, "How do I set up to do that?" and then, "How do I begin? Which foot?" and then, "Oh, there's music? What music?!"

Floor Craft

In addition to learning the basic patterns, the gentleman also has to learn "floor craft"—the art of maneuvering around the dance floor. This is clearly the gentleman's responsibility, and there is very little the lady can do about it. And—it is actually fairly complicated.

In all the smooth/standard dances (waltz, tango, etc.), the gentleman must learn not only to move the couple in the general direction of the line of dance, he must learn the geometry of each of the patterns he leads. These are known as "alignments." He must learn, for example, that right-turning actions should be started facing diagonal to the wall, and left-turning actions facing diagonal to the center of the room, or they will end up going against the line of dance.

The first night our teacher brought in a diagram explaining alignments, Art went and sat down with his head in his hands. He thought he would never learn it! And the teacher thought she would never see him again.

The Latin/rhythm dances are somewhat easier in terms of floor craft because (with some exceptions) they are not expected to move around the line of dance. But these dances can actually present more collision hazards because of the faster speeds at which many of them are danced. And even in these dances, the man must have an understanding of the geometry of the figures he leads in order to choose patterns that will not send his partner crashing into another couple—or the wall!

With all this going through his head, it is no wonder that the man typically has very little attention left over for being responsive to his partner. So it is helpful for the lady to learn responsiveness first, because *somebody* in the partnership has to tune in to what is happening within the couple! In most cases the gentleman will only learn to attune himself to the lady at a much later point, after he has mastered the basics of patterns and floor craft.

> The only test of leadership is that somebody follows.
>
> *Robert K. Greenleaf*

Fear of Crashing

The responsibility for floor craft can make the man fearful, not so much of making a mistake, but of making a mistake that will hurt his partner. His worry about "dire consequences" creates a hesitation in his lead. This hesitancy, in turn, results in failure to give a clear signal to the woman, which she finds confusing. "What does he want me to do?" she thinks. "I'm willing to follow, but I can't figure out what he is leading."

Finally, the fear of crashing is likely to put the gentleman off time. As he hesitates, he misses the beat, and the music goes on without him.

> Football isn't a contact sport; it's a collision sport. Dancing is a contact sport.
>
> *Vince Lombardi*

What If She Won't Go?

Another fear many beginning gentlemen have is that the lady won't "go," when he tries to begin to dance. He's afraid because she is standing right in front of him and he's a nice guy—he doesn't want to hurt her by stepping all over her. A common method used by many beginning dancers to try to solve this problem is to hold their partner at arm's length, figuring that this is safer. Actually, it is more difficult for the lady to feel where her partner is at a distance. If the inside of the lady's right leg is in contact with the inside of the gentleman's right leg, they each know where the other one is, and they really cannot step on each other because their feet are safely out of the way. But this type of close contact raises another problem: at first, this feels like a really rude invasion of your partner's personal space! And out in public, too! (But more about this in Chapter 7.)

For now, let us just say that the gentleman's fear of hurting the lady has two parts: he may hurt her by crashing her into someone else; or he may hurt her by stepping on her, himself. Neither of these fears helps him assume a confident air of leadership.

Issues for the Lady

The biggest initial struggle for most women is the whole idea of following, especially as teachers typically teach the men and women their parts separately. If the lady has learned to do her part, she just wants to do it, and if her partner doesn't "lead" it in a way that makes it easy for her to do what she has been taught, she then has two problems: who to follow and how to follow.

Who to Follow

Remember Bob and Carol from Chapter 1? They were learning the waltz box in their first dance class. The teacher had all the ladies line up on one side of the room, and all the gentlemen on the other. Then she taught the ladies their part and had them all do it at the same time, as they copied her, "Back, side, together, forward, side together."

The teacher then repeated this with the gentlemen, having them do their parts as they copied her, "Forward, side together, back side together." Then she said, "OK, now take your partner and do the step together."

So Carol and Bob got into dance position and tried to do the basic waltz box. Carol knew that she was supposed to "follow," but she also knew she was supposed to be practicing the step they had just learned. If she "followed" Bob, she felt she would be doing something else. Who was she supposed to follow: Bob, or the teacher who said to practice the waltz box?

This is a constant dilemma for women in lessons. If they try to practice the patterns they are being taught, then they are not necessarily "following"—not if their partners are doing something else.

This is made even more complicated because the answer to the question, "Who should I follow?" is not always the same. There are times when the teacher wants the lady to try to do her half of the new pattern, because if she does her part correctly, it may "back lead" the man and help him learn his part. But at other times, the teacher wants the lady to truly respond to what is being led so that the gentleman is getting accurate feedback about his lead.

In a social dance situation, of course, the lady should simply follow to the best of her ability. But in a lesson, she may have to ask the teacher, when she feels confused, "What should I follow? What I hear you saying, or what I feel my partner doing?"

How to Follow

The much bigger issue for the lady, however, is learning *how* to follow. With so much going on, what should she pay attention to? Where does the lead come from? Should she be noticing the man's arms and hands? Does the lead come from his right hand pushing her, his left arm pulling her, or perhaps his feet?

From the point of view of the woman, learning to dance with a partner who also doesn't know how to dance is like learning to play tennis with a partner who is also a beginning tennis player.

He serves the ball; you can't return it. You serve the ball; he can't return it. It's pretty frustrating.

> Dance is communication, and so the great challenge is to speak clearly, beautifully, and with inevitability.
>
> *Martha Graham*

Just as taking lessons from a tennis pro will improve your game faster, taking private lessons from a dance pro can help both the lady and the gentleman learn faster because dancing with a skilled partner can help you get the feeling of what it's "supposed to feel like." And what will you feel? If your dance teacher is any good, you will feel good posture and movement that invites you to come along but does not attempt to force you to do anything.

We have heard people say, "Don't dance with a teacher! If you dance with a teacher, you will never be satisfied with your own spouse!" This is like saying you shouldn't listen to Itzak Perlman play the violin when you are taking violin lessons because he will always be better. Well, yes, it's probably true that you will never play as well as a world-famous *maestro*, but if you give up playing because a professional musician is better, you will never have the pleasure of making your own music. And if your relationship is so shaky that it is threatened by dancing with a better dancer, then you have other problems, far more serious than dancing...

Just as it will take the gentleman time to learn to "lead," it will take the lady time to learn to "follow." Both partners must be patient with each other and with themselves as they embark upon a journey of learning together how to communicate with their bodies. If they build on a foundation of respect and responsibility, they will, over time, achieve heightened responsiveness. Ultimately, "leading and following" will be replaced by collaboration.

Review of Bronze Level Responsiveness: Leading and Following

Gender role issues then and now—rethinking the meaning of "leading"

* The "brute strength" lead does not work (it is disrespectful).
* The "move yourself" system works (each partner takes responsibility).
* Moving yourself requires attunement to your partner (responsiveness).
* Each partner takes turns supplying power; "he goes, she goes" requires **respect, responsibility,** and **responsiveness.**

Issues for the gentleman—man as "slow learner"

* Being required to lead when you feel unsure
* The challenge of multitasking—floor craft, timing and patterns
* Fears of collision or stepping on partner

Issues for the lady—being the "slow learner's" partner

* Who and how to follow—be patient, seek information, and practice your own part

Chapter 5

REALITY CHECK: TAKING CARE
OF YOUR BODY

Yes, dancing is a sport, as well as an art form. It makes very real physical demands on the body. Do you remember your first dance lesson? Do you recall how your arms ached as you tried to hold them in dance position for an hour without leaning on your partner? In Chapter 2 we advised projecting your positive attitude of self-respect physically. "Stand up and smile!" we said. What we didn't say was that standing and moving with good posture will make some parts of your body ache in unfamiliar ways—more so if you normally spend most of your time sitting in a chair.

> First comes the sweat. Then comes the beauty if you're very lucky and have said your prayers.
>
> *George Balanchine*

So now that we have laid out the fundamentals of the **3 Rs of Relationship Fitness** we need to pause for a reality check on the physical side of dancing—a discussion of the fundamentals of caring for your body.

Respecting Your Body

Just as a pianist cannot play beautifully on a piano that is out of tune, a dancer cannot perform beautifully without a well-tuned body. Our bodies are our instruments. We must treat them with care and consideration. Don't take your body for granted—

it is the only one you will be issued in this life. (Despite the fact that some replacement parts are available, most of us would prefer to stick with our original equipment...as long as we can.)

Thanks to immunizations, antibiotics, and the high general level of public sanitation, most people in the developed world today have the good fortune to be healthy when they are young. This makes it easy to take health for granted. When you are young, you can eat anything you want, stay up until all hours, smoke, drink too much coffee or alcohol, and still feel pretty good a day or two later.

But bad habits eventually take their toll. It is amazing how much younger a person in their 50s or 60s looks and feels if they have had life-long good health habits, compared to someone of the same age who has abused their body or taken it for granted.

> Life is a succession of lessons which must be lived to be understood.
>
> *Helen Keller*

Young people who are involved in sports get plenty of good advice from their coaches about the need to be respectful of their bodies, but, sadly, this advice is too often ignored. Pick up the sports section of a newspaper on any day and you can find stories about young athletes who are throwing away promising careers in sport by abusing substances.

Partnered dancing is a team sport. So like the football player who is hung over the morning of the big game, if you fail to take care of your physical needs you harm not just yourself but the team as well. Taking care of your physical needs is part of your responsibility as a dancer for your half of the partnership.

The older you are, the more important this advice is. If you are 25 or older, your physical power is already declining, unless you take action to reverse the decline. Happily, recent studies on aging show that you can at least slow and possibly reverse this process, even if you are 80 or 90!

> You can't turn back the clock. But you can wind it up again.
>
> *Bonnie Prudden*

Sweet Dreams

The good news about caring for your body is that you already know what to do. Use common sense. Get enough sleep. Individual needs vary, but most people need about eight hours of sleep a night to feel really good. If you are exercising hard, you may need additional rest.

We all know this, but we don't do it. So we walk around every day sleep deprived. Sometimes it's hard to admit that mother's old-fashioned advice was good advice. Yet research study after study reinforces the importance of sleep. One study found that volunteers who got eight hours of sleep were three times more likely than sleep-deprived participants to figure out a hidden rule for solving math problems. A few years earlier the same group published a study showing that performance on a test of fine motor skills was significantly improved by adequate sleep. By now we have documented evidence that adequate sleep improves performance on a variety of tests—of memory, concentration, problem solving, and attention—as well as reducing depression and irritability. The simple take-home message is that adequate sleep is crucial for learning, performance, and mood, as well as for energy and physical control.

So if you really want to learn to dance, you probably need more sleep than most people get. Sleep researchers have suggested that not only are most Americans sleep deprived, we have probably been so ever since the invention of the electric light bulb made it possible to stay up after dark!

> Regular naps prevent old age, especially if you take them while driving.
>
> *Anonymous*

Where will you get the extra time for more sleep? You will have to do less of something else, or become more efficient in doing the tasks you are doing now. To decide how to use your time wisely, examine your own values closely. This opens a window into just one of the many fascinating ways in which dancing can change your life for the better.

Speaking for ourselves, the easiest way to find extra time is to turn off the television. Women, especially women with children at home, tend to be more sleep deprived than men. If you are one of these women, a re-evaluation might help you realize that you are trying to be Supermom. You are probably doing too much. What can you simplify? What chores can other family members do? Where can you let go of some of your perfectionism and adopt more reasonable standards in order to be more relaxed and enjoy life more? If your dance partner is your husband, he will be motivated to help you decide how to streamline so you can be a happier and more energetic dance partner.

> Work to become, not to acquire.
>
> *Confucius*

Garbage In, Garbage Out

Decide to take seriously the idea that, "you are what you eat." A diet of junk food results in a body that feels like junk.

Make friends with fresh fruits and vegetables. Most people these days are aware of nutritional recommendations to eat "five-a-day," a *minimum* of five servings of fruits and vegetables daily. (You can count juice for one of these, as long as it is *real* juice.) Eat a variety of foods. One popular system uses different colors as a reminder to eat a variety of foods—red, yellow, green, orange and blue.

Substitute whole grains for more highly refined grains (for example, brown rice instead of white rice; whole grain breads and cereals instead of refined grains). Decrease fat in your diet by simple measures such as removing the skin from chicken before eating it, using less butter and oil in cooking, eating more fish and less red meat, and choosing tomato-based, rather than cream-based sauces for pasta. Just making these few simple changes will improve the healthfulness of your intake without any fancy or complicated diets.

Of course, if you have a medical condition, such as diabetes, follow medical advice about your individual nutritional needs. The guidelines we give here are for people whose health is good.

Like all athletes, dancers need more calories than sedentary people. Dancing uses a lot of energy—this makes us hungry! When we found ourselves eating pizza at midnight at a dance competition, we knew we had really become dancers.

If you become involved in competitive dancing, you will need to plan your eating so that you don't experience an "energy drop" just when you need energy to perform, but we will save that discussion for Chapter 10.

Watch out for harmful substances. Don't overdo the caffeine, especially if you tend to be "hyper." If you drink alcohol, do so in moderation, and **never** before you dance. If you do drugs, cut that out. And please, please, don't smoke or chew tobacco. (When you quit, you will have more energy, enjoy the taste of food more, and your partners will appreciate your lack of tobacco odor. You can then spend the money you save on more dance lessons.)

Water Babies

Hydrate. The average adult body is 55 percent to 75 percent water. Typically, adults lose about 10 cups of water daily; therefore, 8 to 12 cups of fluids should be consumed by everyone in a normal day. You may get up to half this amount in foods without noticing it, but you have to drink the rest.

Like all athletes, dancers lose more water through perspiration during exercise than the average sedentary person, and this fluid loss has to be replaced. The better your physical condition, the more you will sweat, and you will begin to sweat sooner, at a lower body temperature—your body's way of cooling you down.

Fluids play a key role in the cycle of energy production. Blood carries oxygen and glucose to the muscle cells where they are used to produce energy, and carries metabolic waste products away. Since fluid loss reduces blood volume, your heart must work harder when you are dehydrated. Your fluid and electrolyte balance is also thrown off by dehydration, which has potential negative effects on all body and brain functions. Finally, adequate hydration protects your body tissues during the jostles and jolts of physical exercise. If you are focusing strongly on your dancing you may not notice your body's signals that you are thirsty, so hydrate consciously.

Fluid loss not only increases with exercise, it also increases with age. After age 60 or so, the kidneys become less efficient in their ability to concentrate urine, which is why older people have to urinate more frequently.

Even 2 percent dehydration impairs physical performance. Dehydration also impairs thought processes, so you are more likely to make an error in evaluating your situation if you do not hydrate sufficiently. This can contribute to irritability which you may then take out on your dance partner or yourself. Neither is helpful to your dancing.

During a summer whitewater rafting trip in a desert environment, we had an unforgettable experience that taught us the effect of dehydration on mood. Art recalls: We were on a perfectly wonderful rafting trip, but I began to feel irritable. I wasn't having fun. In the middle of an awesomely beautiful wilderness I wanted to go home.

I began to complain to one of our guides, who responded by handing me water. "Drink!" he said. After I had drunk a full quart of water, I suddenly began to feel better. The sky had been blue and the scenery stunning all along, but I had thunderclouds in my brain until I became re-hydrated. The moral of the story is: If you feel grumpy, drink water!

The *American Dietetic Association's Complete Food and Nutrition Guide* gives the following recommendations for hydration with strenuous physical activity (p. 534):

- 2 to 2-½ hours before the activity drink at least 2 cups of nonalcoholic fluids;

- Just before the activity drink 2 cups of water or sports drink;
- Every 15 minutes during the activity drink ½ cup of water or a sports drink.

Carry a water bottle with you. It doesn't have to be fancy bottled water; tap water is fine, too. Supplement this with other liquids as you prefer. Skim milk is an excellent calcium source. Some people like sports liquids, others hate the taste. Choose real fruit juices in preference to "juice flavored" punches, but be aware of the high sugar content of both.

Until very recently, caffeinated beverages were considered a hydration minus due to their diuretic effect (they make you pee). But recent research has indicated that you have to drink a great deal of strong coffee before this becomes a problem. If you drink moderate amounts of coffee or tea, you can count them as fluids. Do be aware, however, of your individual caffeine tolerance. Although caffeinated beverages can make people feel more alert, too much caffeine can make us jittery. Not only does individual tolerance for caffeine vary, tolerance often decreases with age, so even a small amount of caffeine may produce a strong effect in an older person.

Just Say "No"

Alcohol should be avoided before and while dancing not only because of its diuretic effect, but because it is a depressant. By dulling brain centers it impairs alertness, concentration, coordination, response time, judgment, visual perception, and balance—all key elements in dancing. Alcohol places extra stress on the liver, which works to detoxify the alcohol. This can cause early fatigue by interfering with the liver's job of forming extra blood glucose for prolonged physical activity.

And have you ever been on a dance floor with other people who have had too much to drink? It is a very unpleasant experience. People who have no dance training often imagine they dance better when they have had a few drinks. In fact, what the alcohol does is help them decrease their inhibitions about dancing. They no longer worry how they will look to others, so they are able to believe that drinking helps their dancing.

Just the opposite is true. They flail around without any control, which makes them hazardous, not only to their partner, but to other couples on the floor. One or two experiences of getting shoved or kicked by a drunk on the dance floor are enough to make many people think that dancing is no fun. One of the great advantages of dancing at a studio-sponsored or amateur dance club–sponsored dance is that these events are usually alcohol and smoke free. What a pleasure to dance in an environment where everyone is behaving appropriately and you can breathe!

And, need we say it? Never drink before a dance lesson. Because of the effects of alcohol on the brain, you might just as well throw your money away. You won't be able to benefit from the lesson because of the deleterious effects of alcohol on your mental and physical functioning. This will irritate both your partner and your teacher. Later, you won't be able to remember what you were taught, and this will undermine your confidence in your ability to learn.

It should be obvious that recreational drugs, including tobacco, have no place in the life of an athlete. Substance use dissipates your power. Why discard so casually what you work so hard to achieve? Unfortunately, too many dancers still smoke. The adverse effects of smoking are, by now, so well known that we will not belabor this point. Aside from long-term benefits to health and appearance, you will have more energy and more lung power if you stop smoking. And your dance partner will appreciate your improved odor.

Accepting Responsibility for Your Athletic Body

Many of us who come to dancing in middle age have little or no background in athletics. The idea that we need to begin to think of ourselves as dance athletes is a new one, which is hard to get used to. Eating and drinking appropriately are fundamental, but physical power and control also come from physical training.

If you are young and already fairly athletic, you may not need to do anything special to train other than practice your dancing and continue to engage in your other sports. But for those of us who led more sedentary lives before becoming involved with dancing, general fitness training for strength (with weights) and stamina (through aerobic activity) may be needed.

Creating Strength and Stamina

Betty recalls: When I was a bronze dancer a coach asked me, "What do you think you need that would improve your dancing the most?" It was an excellent question. After thinking a bit I was surprised to hear myself answer, "More stamina. I get too tired." Although I had been aware of this at some level, having to answer this question really brought it to the forefront of my consciousness. I was a middle-aged professor who had spent most of my adult years "in my head." If I wanted to dance the swing and the quickstep with good energy and posture, I had to do more than dance to get in shape.

Within a month or two I had another coaching experience that reinforced the point. Former Latin champion Shirley Johnson was telling me to do something with my "lats." "I don't know what you mean," I said. She explained about the latissimus dorsi—back muscles, and demonstrated how she moved hers. "I don't think I have those," I said.

She worked with me until I could feel my "lats," but, along with the other muscles of my back and trunk, they were weak and undeveloped.

These two coaching experiences made me realize that I would not be able to progress as I wished in my dancing unless I improved the power and strength of my instrument—my body. I began working with a fitness trainer.

> No age has a monopoly on success. Any age is the right age to start doing!
>
> **Anonymous**

Fitness training not only improved my strength and stamina, it increased my body awareness. This aided me in following instructions during lessons and coaching to isolate and move various muscle groups. Until I worked on building these muscles I could not recognize the feelings associated with moving them. Increased strength, stamina, and body awareness, in turn, greatly boosted my confidence. I knew I could dance through intense two-hour coaching sessions and multiple call-backs at competitions without feeling like I was going to drop. Eventually, increased strength helped me improve my balance. What a wonderful experience of empowerment!

> Most people miss opportunity because it's dressed in overalls and looks like work.
>
> **Thomas Alva Edison**

Art adds: When I saw how much benefit Betty was getting from fitness training, I decided to work with a trainer, too. Although working out on a regular basis represents an additional significant time and energy commitment, we have both enjoyed the benefits in improved strength and stamina not only in our dancing, but in everyday activities. The feedback from our social environment tells us it is working. I asked for a senior discount for my haircut. The barber said, "You're no senior citizen. I saw the way you sprang up the steps walking in here. Seniors don't move like that!"

If you are a beginning dancer or a strictly social dancer with no interest in competing, you may not want to make the level of commitment represented by fitness training. If you want to have enough energy to dance all night, however, it is a good idea to at least take a brisk walk for 20 minutes a day. Try to walk with good posture, and swing your arms. Walking is an excellent form of exercise that takes no special training or equipment—and it's free! When we're on vacation and not able to get to the gym, we make a point of walking as much as possible, and find we do not experience any loss of leg strength by being away.

Stretch Your Athletic Body

Stretching should be part of every dancer's routine, whether you do additional physical training or not. In dance we are constantly asked to stretch our bodies into more extreme positions than those we use in everyday life. That's how beautiful lines are created. In order to make this possible, and, eventually, comfortable, we must constantly work against the body's tendency to tighten up with exercise.

In *Mind Body Mastery*, world champion gymnast and coach, Dan Millman, refers to the "four Ss of physical talent," which he regards as essential for all athletes: "strength, suppleness, stamina, and sensitivity" (p. 72). Suppleness, "the embodiment of nonresistance" is achieved through stretching.

If you don't know how to stretch, ask your teacher or coach for suggestions. Some studios and health clubs offer classes in stretching. Yoga classes can help by increasing awareness during stretching, and pairing stretching with breathing and relaxation techniques.

You can also browse books and videotapes on stretching to find a system that feels right for you. Millman details the "Peaceful Warrior Four-Minute Warm-Up," which he practices every morning, in *Mind Body Mastery*. The system we routinely use before and after dancing is Mattes', *Active Isolated Stretching*. Betty also likes Brill's, *The Core Program*, which combines exercise and stretching in a workout you can do at home.

The general principle involved in stretching is to move to a slightly more extended range of motion than you are used to, hold the position briefly, and then repeat. There are many different systems of stretching, but one principle they have in common is that you must move gently into the stretch and not force it. This is very important, as it is possible to injure yourself by over-stretching. Watch out for this when you're in a hurry. Rushing makes us more vulnerable to injury by decreasing our mindfulness as we move.

Effective stretching should feel good. Over-stretching feels bad for a reason. Your body is saying, "Back off!"

Relax while stretching, and "breathe into the stretch." As you do this, you'll be able to feel the tightness release. Millman gives a good piece of advice about stretching: "If you ask your body to grow more supple, it will, but you must ask nicely…Your body is like a young child—make courteous, gentle requests, and you'll receive greater cooperation." (p. 83).

> Movement is Life. Life is a process. Improve the quality of the process and you improve the quality of life itself.
>
> *Moshe Feldenkrais*

Pamper Your Athletic Body

Taking responsibility for your newly athletic body is not all work. By all means, find a good massage therapist and schedule massage on a regular basis. Not only does it feel incredible physically, it also makes you feel pampered, which is wonderful for your mental outlook. And notice what every massage therapist tells you at the end of your massage: "Drink plenty of water!"

Caring for your body properly will make you look and feel great. Knowing your body is in good condition will also do wonders for your confidence and optimism.

Review of Reality Check: Taking Care of Your Body

Respect your body, it is your instrument
* Get enough sleep.
* Eat a variety of healthful foods.
* Hydrate, hydrate, hydrate.
* Watch out for harmful substances: alcohol, caffeine, tobacco, and others.

Accept responsibility for your athletic body
* Train for strength and stamina.
* Learn to stretch.
* Pamper your body with massage.

Chapter 6

APPLYING RELATIONSHIP FITNESS SKILLS TO THE DANCE SPAT

As an amateur couple we have had many conversations that go something like this:

"You two dance together?"

"Yes, it's a lot of fun."

"My spouse and I could never do that."

"Why not? You could learn to dance."

"Oh, it's not that we couldn't learn. We took dance lessons, but we quit because we couldn't agree. We nearly killed each other. We decided we'd rather save our marriage."

"Oh, we know what you mean. That is such a common problem that we are actually writing a book about it."

These people believe that because we are both psychologists we never have any problems getting along. If only it were true! We get irritated, impatient, and fed up with each other, just like anyone else. When things are not going well in the dancing, we sometimes feel like quitting. (It seems simpler than homicide.) But these intense times of gloom and doom are less frequent than they used to be. The advantage we do have as psychologists is our belief in change. Our whole profession is based on the premise that people can change. Our clinical work has taught us that when people sincerely "hang in there" and try to solve their problems by openly exploring and revealing how they feel, their relationship shifts away from strife and toward happiness.

Early on, when we began to see our relationship issues unfold on the dance floor, we decided to apply what we already knew about relationships to develop a system that would allow us to practice without hurting each other's feelings and wasting our time. It's not perfect, but it is much, much better than it was. By applying the **3 Rs of Relationship Fitness** you can do this, too.

What Is a Dance Spat?

Unfortunately, a great many couples who think they would like to dance together end up quitting because of their squabbling. In contrast, after reading a draft of Chapter 1, Betty's sister, who dances with her teacher, asked, "What is a dance spat?" Her question showed that she accepts the authority of her teacher and tries to do what is asked of her. She describes her lessons as lots of fun. In such a relationship, there is no such thing as a "dance spat."

> Mistakes are the usual bridge between inexperience and wisdom.
>
> *Phyllis Theroux*

What we call a "dance spat" can happen when there is a problem in the dancing and the partners disagree about what has gone wrong or what to do next. But disagreements can occur frequently and minor problems don't always escalate into a "dance spat." A "dance spat" happens when the disagreement between the partners results in a conversation in which it feels like one partner is trying to be "right" at the expense of the other partner. Angry and hurt feelings and loss of "team spirit" in the partnership are the result.

"Dance spats" most often occur in practice sessions, but they can also happen during lessons or even in a performance.

What About Fighting with Your Teacher?

"Dance spats" are most likely to occur when the partners are at the same status level—both amateurs or both professionals. Dance spats between students and teachers are less common because, by definition, the teacher is always "right," in the sense that he or she is the acknowledged authority in the partnership. This does not mean that there is no such thing as a student who argues with the teacher—far from it! It is very common for students to feel misunderstood by teachers, and for students to be unaware of what they are doing with their bodies as they try to learn. But dance teachers are used to this and, if they are experienced, they often have a variety of effective ways to help students understand what they are trying to teach. These interactions do not turn into what we call "dance spats" because the teacher does not participate in the "spat" as an equal with the student.

In the long run, the student who often argues with the teacher is likely to change teachers, either because the teacher won't put up with their behavior, or because the student finds another teacher. After all, it doesn't make sense to pay someone to teach you and then spend your lesson time arguing with them.

An interesting exception can occur when the student is married to the teacher. In the context of the marital relationship, the student feels more equal to the teacher. We have been shocked, occasionally, to observe some students berating their teacher-spouse at dance competitions. But the stress of competition may, unfortunately, bring out the worst in people—more about that in Chapter 10.

A different type of exception occurs when the teacher is abusive. One highly-publicized dance fight between a teacher and his student allegedly involved his shoving her and calling her a cow at a social dance. She sued him for the very large sum she had paid him in advance—and won. Whether she ever got her money back, we don't know. According to newspaper accounts of this story, it certainly sounded like the teacher was being abusive to his student. The history of the student's prior behavior to the teacher was not covered. In any event, this does not sound like it could have been a happy and satisfying dance partnership. We know that some people do stay in abusive relationships, but why they do is beyond the scope of this book.

For the purpose of our discussion here, the term "dance spat" refers to a disagreement between dance partners that does not involve physical, verbal or mental *abuse*, but results in hurt feelings. If you are in an abusive relationship, you need to get out of it, regardless of how good a dancer your partner is. It just isn't worth it. Remember, dancing is supposed to be fun!

OK, now we hope it is clear that we are not talking about people who beat each other up. We are talking about the way we often get "testy" with a partner when we are trying to do our best and we believe that if our partner would only change, everything would be better. This type of problem occurs, at times, in every close couple relationship. If we can learn to handle this better in the context of dancing, we can use the same skills in every other situation. So let's take a look at a place where dance spats are most likely to occur—the practice session.

The Practice Session

Dance spats often happen during practice sessions because when couples practice on their own there is no teacher or coach present to exert authority and give information about what is needed to fix the problems that inevitably arise in the dancing.

Remember Ted and Alice from Chapter 1? They were the couple who decided to practice at the gym so they wouldn't forget what they learned in each week's lesson.

Within a few minutes after beginning to practice their waltz, Alice complained that Ted was pushing her. Ted felt attacked, so he defended himself. Soon they were blaming each other in an argument—a classic "dance spat." "No, I'm not!" "Yes, you are!"

When this happens, what is being practiced—dancing, or discord? The truth is, what you practice is what you will do. Arguing while trying to practice dancing strengthens the habit of arguing while dancing. This is obviously counterproductive.

> ## Practice makes permanent.
> *Brian Jud*

If Ted and Alice are blaming each other when they dance, they are doing it in other areas of their lives, so dancing has not caused the problem, it has simply revealed it.

Application of the principles established in the first five chapters will prevent many dance spats. On the other hand, life is not perfect, and neither are we. We all make mistakes, so every couple, no matter how compatible, will face the reality of the "dance spat" at least some of the time. Remember the batting average—no one bats 1.000.

Let's review their spat from Chapter 1, analyzing it within the context of the **3Rs of Relationship Fitness**:

Alice complains, "You're pushing me!"

- Respect. Is this a respectful way for Alice to speak to Ted?
- Responsibility. Is Alice taking responsibility for what she perceives is a problem?

- Responsiveness. Is Alice showing an empathic response to Ted?

The answer to all of these would have to be no. "But, wait," we hear you say, "he's not being respectful and responsive to her if he is pushing her!" OK, we understand this, but did we mention how important patience is in this process? Just hold on and we'll get to that. Now it's Ted's turn.

"No, I'm not. I'm hardly touching you!" Ted says.

- Respect. Is this a respectful way for Ted to speak to Alice?
- Responsibility. Is Ted taking responsibility for his half of this interaction?
- Responsiveness. Is Ted being responsive by trying to understand Alice's feedback to him?

Again, the answer is no. Alice has voiced her concern about what she is feeling by attacking Ted. Predictably, he responds to attack with defense. But it gets worse. Alice then retorts with escalation. Recall her next contribution to this interaction:

"Well, to me this is a push!" says Alice, *giving him a little shove.*

With many couples the practice session would be over right then. Alice's response is very disrespectful. Although we can understand her frustration, that doesn't justify her disrespect. The content of her reply shows that she has actually understood that Ted doesn't realize he is being too physical in his attempt to lead her, but this understanding has not resulted in more responsiveness on her part. Although at some level she may be aware that Ted's "pushing" is unintentional, she behaves as if she believes he is doing it on purpose. Her blaming stance is doomed to failure. Angry escalation is not the best way to get an empathic response from your partner.

Luckily, Ted shows more forbearance than many partners and does not counter-escalate. Instead, he says nothing and they try again. But by now he is also angry, so it doesn't take long before he lets go with his next salvo:

"But you don't go if I don't do what you call pushing!" says Ted.

This response shows that Ted has actually listened to what Alice said, and tried to analyze why he is using a level of physicality that she experiences as a push. He has decided that it is because of her lack of response that he is being too physical. This neatly serves to blame Alice—she has produced her own trouble, in effect, by being too unresponsive. So blame is followed by counter-blame.

"Well, I can't tell when you want me to go to promenade, but I don't want to be pushed, either," Alice retorts.

This is more counter-blame, but it is also an accurate representation of what Alice is feeling. Like Ted's comment that she doesn't go if he doesn't push, it is actually a common problem and a great question to take to their next lesson—but they haven't learned this yet.

"Why don't you do it the way the teacher showed you? I don't have any trouble feeling it from him, but he doesn't push."

This is a low blow and Alice knows it. Now she has thrown caution to the winds and is more interested in winning the argument than in solving the problem. To make the unfavorable direct comparison of your partner with another dancer is about as disrespectful as one can get, even if it is obviously true. In fact, it may be worse because it *is* obviously true. Any beginning dancer is going to be less skilled than the teacher, so to bring up this evident fact in the middle of an argument has no real purpose other than to hurt the other person's feelings. Ted falls right into the trap of further counter-escalation.

"So you're saying it's my fault you don't move?" Ted angrily replies. "Other ladies seem able to follow me. Maybe it's you!"

The original, valid enough, content that sparked this spat is now completely lost. Each partner has degenerated to the level of a small child on the playground. The practice session is over and, depending upon how well they get along in general, the argument may deteriorate further and go off into other areas that have nothing to do with dancing. For some couples, recovering from this type of spat may take hours, or even days. So how could the problem have been handled better?

Learn to Use "I-Messages"

Respect and responsibility come neatly together in the simple but uncommon practice of using what Thomas Gordon has called, "I-Messages." (See: *Parent Effectiveness Training*). Because we are all immersed in our own points of view, we humans have a tendency to communicate our perceptions, ideas, and opinions as if they were facts. When those perceptions, ideas, and opinions have to do with another person, we tend to express these with "you messages":

"You are pushing me."

"You won't move."

"You are a brute."

"You are overly sensitive."

And so on.

Each time we send a "you message," there is great danger the recipient may experience this as a criticism. If they feel criticized, they are likely to respond with a defense. Remember we said in Chapter 1 that dancing is an activity that tends to assault our psychological defenses?

But when we express our perceptions, ideas, and opinions as, "I-Messages," it shows that we are taking responsibility for the communication and that we do not regard it as fact. This turns out to be much more respectful to the listener and much easier to receive. If the communication is registered, rather than defended against, there is a chance it may be understood and even responded to in a positive way. But even if it is not understood, the "I-Message" invites dialog, rather than shutting it off. This is most likely to be a useful approach to communication in any shared enterprise. Consider how different this feels:

"I'm experiencing something that feels to me like a push."

"I can't seem to figure out how to communicate the lead to you."

"I'm feeling a lot of upper body strength from you. Funny, instead of feeling like I want to move, I'm feeling like I want to resist this."

"Wow, I'm trying to be gentle, but I'm having trouble being delicate enough!"

Let's revisit the interaction between Alice and Ted and see how "I-Messages" might be used to change what happens between them:

Alice thinks, "He's pushing me and I don't like it! How could I rephrase that as an 'I-Message'?" She tries, *"Gosh, Ted, I'm feeling something that feels like a push to me. Do you know what I'm talking about?"*

Here Alice takes responsibility for communicating what she feels and owns it as her experience. She does not accuse Ted of anything and she asks him if he understands what she is trying to communicate.

Ted is less likely to become defensive because he does not feel accused of anything. He thinks and then says, *"Well, I'm not sure. Can you tell me the next time you feel it?"*

Now they are participating as partners in trying to understand something together. They are acting as if they are on the same team.

Let's take a different version of this interaction. Let's say Alice begins as she did before:

"You're pushing me!"

Ted thinks, "That's a 'you message,' but let me try to respond with an 'I-Message'. Maybe I will ask a clarifying question." *"I'm not sure I understand. Can you show me what you mean?"*

Here Ted has ignored the implied accusation of the "you message" and asked a question that invites collaboration.

A Foundation of Respect

You may recall that in Chapter 2 we said, "Since respect is the foundation of any positive relationship, do not choose as a dance partner anyone you feel you can't respect." If you have followed that advice, you will find it helpful to remind yourself of this when you begin to feel irritated with your partner. Your partner is not trying to irritate you. Your partner is trying his or her best to dance properly. If you respect your partner, you can believe in his or her good intentions, even as you are simultaneously amazed that he or she can be repeating the same error *again*! (Like you never made the same mistake more than once?)

Applying Responsibility

So if you can accept that your partner is on your team and trying to dance correctly, even when you feel irritated by repeated errors, how can you apply responsibility to this situation? The answer lies in realizing that you can still try your best to practice fundamental dance skills that always need work.

Your gentleman is messing up the lead in the cha cha? You can always work on your individual posture and foot placement, as he tries to figure out the pattern. Your lady can't seem to follow your lead in the waltz? You can always practice your individual posture and frame, and maybe your heels and toes, if you can remember them.

If you can take responsibility for practicing individual skills *you* need to work on, the practice session will feel less frustrating. Even if you find, as a team, that you cannot make a certain pattern work, you will not have to feel the time and effort were wasted, because, at the very least, you will have been able to practice your individual dance posture and frame, and proper use of the feet.

What about Responsiveness?

Most dance spats occur because we experience what we feel is a failure of responsiveness from our partner. While it is true that we are sometimes irritated because a partner cannot remember their half of the material, this can be handled with a frank admission, "This has gone out of my head. I really can't remember what to do here." When this occurs remember to apply the *Rule of Three* from Chapter 2. Try the move three different ways and if you still can't make it work, write it down and take it to the next lesson. Applying the *Rule of Three* keeps you on the same team. No anger, no blame, no hard feelings. We are both allowed to be imperfect.

But when we feel that our partner is too strong or too unclear in the lead (for ladies) or fails to follow (for gentlemen), we are less likely to be patient and kind. This physical failure to respond leads to irritation, and when we are irritated we are often triggered to react quickly and angrily. If we can teach ourselves to delay that immediate response, we have the opportunity to recapture responsiveness in the partnership. Taking a deep breath, moving physically away from your partner, and taking a drink of water are all good strategies that will buy you time to think about what to say and do next.

Reality Check: Your Mental and Physical State

As discussed in Chapter 5, the mental and physical state that you bring to the practice session can have a major impact on your mood. If you are tired, dehydrated, hungry, coming down with a cold, or stressed about something else that is going on in your life, you are more likely to be short on patience and long on irritability. So prepare for your practice session in a realistic way, rather than showing up unprepared.

Practice Preparation Checklist

- No alcoholic beverages or other balance-altering substances before practicing.
- Bring water and drink it.
- Bring a snack if you need it.
- Have appropriate clothing and shoes with you.
- Bring music, boom box, or other items that you and your partner have agreed you would provide.
- Be on time; plan for traffic and parking.
- Leave time for stretching and warm-up before moving into problem areas or working on new choreography.
- Bring a good attitude—cheerful, upbeat, kind and forgiving toward yourself and your partner.
- Put a smile on your face.
- Breathe.

Review of Applying Relationship Skills to the Dance Spat

Use the 3Rs of Relationship Fitness

* Speak and behave respectfully.
* Take responsibility for your own perceptions, communication, and behavior.
* Respond to your partner with kindness and empathy.

Learn to use "I-Messages"

Be aware of your mental and physical state

Be prepared for practice sessions

Silver Level Relationship Fitness—
Congratulations

Chapter 7

SILVER LEVEL RESPECT: DANCING AND ROMANCING

Congratulations! If you have made it this far, trying to put into practice the skills laid out in the previous chapters, you are now ready for the next level of relationship skill: the silver level. As you may know from your dance experience, the transition from bronze to silver is the most difficult transition in ballroom dancing. Many people never get beyond bronze, and that is OK. Bronze is your social dance level; its skills provide a foundation for everything that comes later. These skills need to be practiced again and again, not abandoned as you progress to a higher level. The same is true for bronze relationship skills.

Just as most people are content to learn enough to remain at the bronze level of dance, if you can master bronze level relationship skills, you will have a solid foundation for relationships, which will serve you well: respect, responsibility, and responsiveness. But if you want more, then stay with us as we develop these skills at the next level of complexity. And we will begin to open up some taboo topics in relationships: sex and power. Are you ready?

Is Dancing Romantic?

Most people would say yes. The courtship dance is a long-standing folk tradition across many cultures. There are even courtship dances in the animal kingdom, especially among birds. In several species the male puts on an elaborate courtship display to impress the female and she chooses the best "dancer" as her mate.

> Dancing is the perpendicular expression of a horizontal desire.
>
> *George Bernard Shaw*

Social dancing has been a part of courtship in Western culture for many centuries, eventually evolving into the ballroom dances of today. The lyrics to popular songs highlight the romance of dancing: "Darling, save the last dance for me," "Waltz again with me," "Memories of the dance we shared beneath the stars." Many couples take their first ballroom dance lessons when they are planning to dance at their wedding. And the first dance as man and wife is supposed to symbolize the beauty of their new life together.

In fact, it was the supposed romance of dancing that led to Victorian disapproval of social dancing.

The Victorian Objection

We sometimes forget that partnered dancing was once considered scandalous. When the waltz was first introduced into British upper-class circles at a ball given in London by the Prince Regent in 1816, an editorial in *The Times* blasted it:

> We remarked with pain that the indecent foreign dance called the Waltz was introduced (we believe for the first time) at the English court on Friday last...it is quite sufficient to cast one's eyes on the voluptuous intertwining of the limbs and close compressure on the bodies in their dance, to see that it is indeed far removed from the modest reserve which has hitherto been considered distinctive of English females. So long as this obscene display was confined to prostitutes and

adulteresses, we did not think it deserving of notice; but now that it is attempted to be forced on the respectable classes of society by the evil examples of their superiors, we feel it a duty to warn every parent against exposing his daughter to so fatal a contagion....We know not how it has happened (probably by the recommendation of some worthless and ignorant French dancing-master) that so indecent a dance has now been exhibited at the English court...we trust it will never again be tolerated in any moral English society (Stephenson and Iaccarino, pp. 14–15).

Geez, don't hold back! Hard to believe that now the English are considered among the foremost ballroom dancers in the world, with world titles routinely won and held by English couples for many years.

As the popularity of partnered dancing grew, the concern about immorality persisted. Typical of this nineteenth-century concern are the comments from the pastor of Saint Paul's Lutheran Church in New York City in 1883:

Dancing has made many homes desolate. It has engendered jealousy in many households; it has ruined many lives and has brought death to many doors. Go to a dancing club, look at the flushed faces, see the attire of the women, mark the looks and gestures of the dancers, hear their words, and then tell me if dancing is God-like... No husband cares to see his wife in another's arms... (Stephenson and Iaccarino, pp. 12–13).

Just as with changing fashions in music, as each new dance was introduced (for example, the tango, the Charleston, the Lindy hop), the new dance became the focus of concern about immorality while the older dances acquired respectability. Yet, despite the fact that very few parents today are worried that learning the waltz will lead to the downfall of their children, there are still religious groups that forbid dancing on the grounds that the touching between men and women, which is a routine part of social dancing, promotes immorality.

> Sex in a dance is in the eyes of the beholder.
>
> *Gwen Verdon*

We experienced this when we visited Morocco. We were staying in a hotel that catered to Western tourists. To our pleasure and surprise a rather good combo was playing dance tunes during dinner. We asked our tour guide whether it would be all right for us to get up and dance. He frowned, "We don't do that here," he said.

Romance and the Dance Lesson

Yes, ballroom dancing involves close physical contact, which can make it very romantic if you and your partner are "in sync" with each other and dancing well. When you are experiencing that attunement, it is a truly wonderful feeling of being in the moment together.

> When everything is working, dancing is better than sex.
>
> *Rosendo Fumero*

But in order to learn to dance well, you have to take lessons. And dance lessons are **not** a romantic experience.

As we pointed out in Chapter 1, dance lessons often make people feel anxious. Otherwise competent adults tend to feel like they don't know what they are doing when they walk into a dance studio. We worry about how we look to others and what they will think of us—kind of like a first date, come to think of it. So maybe it is a bit like courtship, after all—in the very early stages...

Respecting Your Partner's Space

One of the really weird things about dancing is that the very thing that makes it appear romantic to the onlooker creates a major problem for the dancer—the close physical contact between partners. Think about it. If you go to a social dance venue and watch untrained dancers attempting a "slow dance," what do you see? Couples cling to each other in a semi bear-hug with their upper bodies, but then their feet have no space. Because they are trying not to step on each other, they pull their pelvis back and shuffle from foot to foot. This position produces a lot of stress on the upper body, causing each member of the couple to disturb the balance of their partner. With poor balance, they are falling over, so they lean even harder on each other. Watching this makes our backs hurt. No wonder they find dancing exhausting!

When we are first learning to dance, the crowding problem in the dance partnership is addressed in two ways: (1) the initial hold that is taught is farther apart, with contact at the level of arms, shoulders, and hands; and (2) the lady is offset to the gentleman's right (her left), so that there is room for the moving leg of the person dancing forward (man or woman) to swing between the legs of the partner. With increased proficiency, dancers are allowed to move closer so that the lady's right hip/torso and the gentleman's right hip/torso are in contact. This makes possible higher-level figures with more rotation, such as pivots. Without such close contact, it is impossible for the partners to get around each other. In other words, we have to move closer together in order to get out of each other's way!

The physics of partnered dancing is truly counterintuitive. Without training, we want to pull our hips away to create more space. It also seems more respectful to the partner. But, in fact, the opposite is true. We actually create more space for our partner by bringing the hips very close so that we can feel the partner's moving leg and respond with the correspondingly appropriate movement. Rather, it is taking the head far away from the partner and stretching it toward the left, together with shaping the torso-shoulder complex, that creates space in the partnership and, with that space, the freedom to dance.

Confusing Messages

A great deal of communication is nonverbal. It is not only what we say, it is how we behave that sends signals to others about our thoughts, feelings, and intentions. It is easy to think of many examples. Much of comedy, for instance, is based on a contradiction between the content and the tone, emphasis, or timing of what is said.

Ballroom dancing seems to send a romantic message. Dancing portrays romance to the observer. But we don't always intend to convey romance to every partner. Sometimes (many times) we just want to enjoy dancing. This contradiction can feel confusing when we are taking dance lessons. The physical actions necessary to accomplish the dance do not mean what they would mean if we were in a different (non-dancing) context. To illustrate the point, let's take an example that has nothing to do with dancing.

If you go to the doctor and you are asked to disrobe, you are not surprised or confused by this request. But the fact that you feel it is all right to take off your clothes at a medical appointment is not an accident. The "choreography" of the physical examination has been carefully thought out to distinguish this interaction from the only other type of interaction (outside of a nudist colony or locker room) in which an adult is naked in the presence of another adult—the marital or sexual encounter.

There are several elements that signal the fact that a physical exam is not a sexual encounter: the patient disrobes in private, not while the doctor is watching; the patient dons a very asexual garment—the hospital gown; the doctor wears a white coat, which sends the message that this is a medical encounter; the doctor uncovers only one part of the patient's body at a time, making sure to cover the rest (this is called "draping" and is part of clinical training); the doctor uses formal technical language in speaking to the patient; and the doctor carries a stethoscope or other equipment that symbolizes the medical nature of the encounter.

Now think of the dance lesson. Does anything symbolize that the close touching of bodies is not romantic? Not really. Not in any organized, systematic way. In fact, dancing is culturally promoted as being romantic.

No wonder so many people feel confused and uncomfortable about dancing with anyone other than their spouse or sweetheart. Yet to take lessons means you have to dance with the teacher and, in most studios, with other students. You have to test your skills in social dancing situations: Can he really lead? Can she really follow? You can't find this out unless you dance with someone other than your regular partner. If you can only dance with one person, you haven't really learned to dance, you have learned a routine.

The close physical contact required to dance in synchrony with another person is part of what makes dancing seem romantic, but it involves a level of body contact that we normally allow only for our special someone, or for hugging a close friend or relative.

> Dance is the only sport I know where a man can touch a woman over most parts of her body, and she thanks you for it afterwards.
>
> *Mario Robau*

To add to the confusion, many single people *do* learn to dance in order to meet a potential romantic partner. We know several couples who met through social dancing and went on to get married. Does that mean you shouldn't go social dancing if you are not interested in meeting someone for the purpose of romance? That hardly seems fair. Dancing is fun in and of itself, and not everyone goes social dancing looking for romance. In fact, we know people who go social dancing without their spouse because their spouse doesn't dance. This doesn't necessarily mean that their marriage is in trouble.

We have also heard from single women who want to learn to dance but aren't looking for a date. The social dance presents a problem. One woman told us that her dance teacher kept recommending that she attend the studio dance party so she could practice what she was learning in her private lessons. She didn't know how to explain that she just didn't want to face the inevitable invitation to go out for coffee or drinks afterward. She just wanted to dance, nothing more. Rather than facing the social advances she anticipated, she never did attend a social dance, and eventually, she dropped out.

The "singles" dance helps to serve as a signal that meeting a potential romantic partner is one purpose of the event. Unfortunately, we did get in trouble over this one time. Looking for a place to dance in a strange city, we unwittingly ended up at a singles dance. When Art left to go to the restroom, a stranger asked Betty to dance. Upon Art's return, the stranger was angry to discover that Betty was married! Moral: if you are married, avoid attending singles dances—it only serves to confuse potential partners.

Violating Personal Space

A half-century ago, Hall coined the term *proxemics* to describe the distances between people during social interactions. He found that physical distance mirrored interpersonal distance. Furthermore, he found strong cultural differences in the physical distances with which people were comfortable in social interactions. (The Japanese movie *"Shall We Dance?"* is based on the conflict between the traditional Japanese taboo on touching and the physical closeness required to learn to ballroom dancing.)

> Like gravity, the influence of two bodies on each other is inversely proportional not only to the square of their distance but possibly even the cube of the distance between them.
>
> *Edward T. Hall*

Depending upon our own ethnic and cultural background, the closeness required for partnered dancing can feel like a violation of our own space or of our partner's space, even when we are dancing with our own spouse. This aspect of dancing can create a great deal of discomfort. Learning to violate another person's physical boundaries, and allowing them to violate yours, is one of the greatest challenges facing the person who wants to learn to dance—and one that is rarely openly confronted. When the relationship is based on respect, however, it is possible to maintain appropriate interpersonal boundaries.

When we were coached by former Canadian Champion Pierre Allaire, he told us that he regards it as a privilege whenever a lady, including his own wife, allows him to set up in a closed dance position. By maintaining a conscious awareness that this is a privilege, he conveys respect for each partner. The gentlemanly and sophisticated dancing for which he is well known has always been wildly popular with audiences. People can see respect, as well as grace, portrayed in motion.

So think about the very first step in any dance for which you set up in a closed dance position. The man typically begins by stepping forward, into the spot where his partner is standing. How rude is that! And when the woman goes forward, she has to do the same. Normally we do not stand that close to another person unless we are going to hug them or fight with them, or we are in a crowded elevator or train, in which case we usually don't face them. Yes, in order to dance, we have to overcome years of cultural training about the rules regarding respect for another person's physical boundaries.

So there are really two complicated issues that can cause confusion when we are asked to step into the space in which our partner is standing. We feel like we are violating our partner's personal space, which can feel rude or sexual. Or maybe it feels rude because it seems sexual. There are many possibilities.

But whatever they are for you, you can be sure that your dance teacher has not been trained to deal with them.

Training for Closeness

As clinical psychologists we have a background of experience that provides an interesting analogy to the physical boundary violation that is a routine aspect of ballroom dancing. Therapists are expected to violate the normal boundaries of social interaction in a different way—emotionally, rather than physically. In a normal social interaction, people respect the privacy of others by using a variety of maneuvers designed to keep the conversational partner from becoming uncomfortable. Most common among these are avoiding sensitive topics, refraining from asking nosy personal questions, providing reassurance with general upbeat statements, and changing the subject when we sense that the other person is experiencing (or is about to experience) negative emotions.

Therapists are trained to do just the opposite. We must ask nosy personal questions, bring up sensitive and difficult topics, refrain from providing superficial reassurance, and delve into areas that produce negative emotions. Student therapists have to work hard to overcome their cultural programming in order to bear their own discomfort about making another person uncomfortable. Over time they must learn to become increasingly calm in the presence of the discomfort of others. Therapists can violate the normal rules of social interaction because we have special permission to do so—the patient is coming to us for help. And as part of the contract, we assure the patient of confidentiality.

A further part of the training of therapists is to learn that when we violate the usual norms of social discourse, we can expect patients to react differently than they would to a neighbor or friend to whom they might tell their troubles. Patients often develop stronger feelings about their therapists, both positive and negative, than about other people they know. Sometimes those feelings take the form of a sexual attachment. Sometimes they result in intense anger. Student therapists need to learn not to be taken by surprise when this happens, and to explore these feelings openly with the patient, just as they would any other feelings that come up in the course of therapy.

Dance teachers must violate the normal boundaries of social interaction physically, rather than emotionally. But they have no special training to help them expect and deal with the confusing emotions that they and their students may experience when they must accept physical closeness from a stranger in order to learn to dance.

The traditional approach to teaching dancing tried to handle this problem nonverbally, signaling distance by using heightened formality. Studios used formal titles for everyone (such as Miss and Mr.), and teachers were forbidden to give their last names. Sometimes they did not use their real first names. Teachers traditionally dressed formally, in coats and ties, dresses and heels, and students were encouraged to do the same. Today, most of these practices have fallen away. As society, in general, has become more informal, the dance studio has also become a less formal setting. And, with the rise of the independent (non-franchise) dance studio, many dance professionals are now on their own, more than ever, in trying to figure out what to do to help students handle the potentially confusing messages embedded in violating the personal space of others, when all they really want to do is dance.

> There are only two places where indiscriminate hugging is tolerated: the brothel and the ballroom.
>
> *M. A. Ham*

The Crush

The traditional rules in the dance studio of 30 or 40 years ago had two intended functions: (1) to reassure students that dancing was a respectable activity (in case they had those Victorian ideas); and (2) to protect teachers from being stalked by the student who might develop a crush on them. Even in the days when the dance lesson was more formal, teachers have always had to deal with students who develop a crush on the teacher. What's that all about?

The crush often surprises the person who develops it as much as it does the person on the receiving end. We are not saying that true romance never can develop between a dance teacher and a student; indeed, we know of several cases where this has happened. But, let's face it, a dance professional teaches a lot of students. It is not realistic to think the teacher will reciprocate every crush.

Why do these crushes develop? There are many reasons. First, the dance teacher is generally a pleasant, and often a charming, person. The dance business depends on good salesmanship, and the personality of the teacher is a big factor in the success of sales. To make the initial sale and keep the customer coming back for more lessons, the dance professional should be selling a fun experience. A secondary, but still important, part of the teacher's appeal ought to be a personal appearance that is clean, well-groomed, and attractively dressed. Dancing is a visual art— the teacher ought to be easy to look at. A good dance teacher has excellent posture and knows how to move gracefully, adding to the visual appeal that may promote a crush.

Many dance teachers offer the glow of youth in their appeal. Often there is a significant age difference between the customer with the crush and the teacher. Older students, most especially, may have romantic associations with dancing that date back to the days of their high school prom.

The crush is also promoted by the respectful and interested way the teacher treats the student. Many people feel that no one listens to them or takes them seriously. The dance teacher who will listen to your stories and laugh at the jokes your spouse was sick of hearing 30 years ago is an attractive individual, indeed.

In a beginning class it is, of course, a lot more fun to dance with the teacher than with anyone else because no one else really knows what they are doing. If you dance with the teacher, you may have a prayer of getting it right and having a successful experience on the dance floor! This adds to the teacher's popularity as a dance partner and may help to promote the crush. We have heard of situations at a studio dance party where students have kept track of how many times the teacher danced with each student, and were angry if favoritism appeared to be shown—to the point of asking later, "How come you danced with her three times and with me only twice!" Oh, my.

Most important, however, in promoting the development of a crush, is the physical closeness that is a requirement of partnered dancing. We simply associate that level of touching with romance. Married adults are not used to being touched by anyone other than their spouse. The dance lesson presents them with an experience of physical proximity to a member of the opposite sex that they have not experienced since their dating days. And unmarried adults experience this level of physical closeness outside the dance studio only in the context of dating.

Married or single, it can be disconcerting in this situation to find your heart going "pitty-pat" at the touch of a stranger, when your head knows perfectly well that this makes no sense.

> There is a bit of insanity in dancing that does everybody a great deal of good.
>
> *Edwin Denby*

Dance teachers need to learn to not be taken by surprise when they see evidence that a student is developing a crush on them. And it is not a good idea for the teacher to try to become less attractive in an attempt to head off the crush (for example, making rude remarks, dressing poorly, coming late to lessons). These behaviors are just bad for business in the long run, and will only help to select for crushes those students whose psychological dynamics attract them to abusive relationships.

For most students, the crush is simply a phase that they get over with more exposure. As people become more experienced in partnered dancing, they become much more interested in the technical proficiency of their partner, rather than in any imaginary romance. Could he/she lead/follow? Did he/she stay over on his/her own side and over his/her own feet?

Rather than trying to keep crushes from developing, it makes more sense for teachers to remain polite and respectful in their treatment of students and to think carefully about ground rules for everyone that will promote ladylike and gentlemanly behavior in the dance studio. For those few students who do not handle their crushes well, it may be necessary to take them aside and calmly explain the parameters of the relationship (for example, "I'm your teacher, not your date." "You may not touch me in that way.") The assistance of a more experienced dance professional can be very helpful in such a situation.

If a student cannot accept the boundaries that are clearly set forth, he/she may have to be asked to leave, which is a shame. (This is, by the way, one of the best reasons for avoiding complicated financial entanglements between dance professionals and their students. Students who invest a lot of money up front may have the idea that they are buying more than is realistic to suppose. And dance pros who are heavily in debt to students may have difficulty setting appropriate and reasonable boundaries.)

Closeness and Inhibition

While the physical closeness of bodies and the touching required for ballroom dancing can promote crushes and boundary violations from some students, among other students, similar feelings of closeness or sexuality may produce inhibition.

For partners in love, although close physical contact while dancing can be a distraction at first, dancing can ultimately become a new avenue for expressing deep feelings. But for partners in less close social relationships, the physical contact required for partnered dancing can lead to psychological and physical inhibition, which interfere with the expressiveness of their dancing.

Both men and women must be willing to face these issues, and to develop productive strategies to overcome inhibitions if they want to continue enjoying their dancing.

For some women, a gay partner presents the perfect solution to these problems. There are so many advantages. She doesn't have to worry about developing feelings other than friendship for him; she can share a room with him at a competition; and she doesn't have to deal with the jealousy of her boyfriend or spouse toward her dance partner.

But this is not a realistic strategy for everyone. For most students it is probably the behavior of the dance professionals they work with that will eventually help them understand and believe that Latin hip motion, for example, is simply a technique, not an invitation to intimacy. The pros set the tone in any given studio. If they treat dancing as a fun activity, and if they show by their behavior that they do not confuse dancing with romance, most students will gradually relax and become less inhibited over time.

So, Is It Romantic?

In the end, only some of the time, and probably mostly not. People at lower levels of proficiency are actually more likely to be having a "romantic" experience than someone who is a better dancer, because the higher-level dancer is more likely to be thinking about technique or floor craft, rather than just enjoying the dance. Dancing is also much more romantic to the onlooker than to the performer, and this is truer the better you get. If you ask top dance pros what they are thinking about while portraying romance on the dance floor they will say things like, "the music," or "the choreography," or, "When do I get to eat?"

And while romantic partnerships may break up, respectful partnerships often endure for many years.

Review of Silver Level Respect: Dancing and Romancing

Is dancing romantic?
* Conflicting cultural ideas.
* The idea of dancing is more romantic than the reality.
* Dance lessons are not romantic.

Respecting your partner's space

* The counterintuitive physics of dance—give each other space by moving closer together.

Confusing messages and violating personal space

* Some dancers are looking for romance; some just want to dance.
* The closeness and movement of dance can send the wrong message or produce inhibition.

Training for closeness and the crush

* Dance teachers are not trained to handle the confusing emotions stirred up by dancing.

Chapter 8

SILVER LEVEL RESPONSIBILITY: ACTIVE LEARNING

In Chapter 3 we discussed the basic bronze level of responsibility: dance only your own half of the partnership by staying over your own feet and on your own side. We stressed the importance of "minding your own business"—just dance, and let the teacher teach. Don't "help" by trying to teach your partner. We said that the most important thing you can do to be helpful to your partner is to do your own part as well as you can.

Taking responsibility for learning to do your own part as well as you can is the focus in this chapter as we advance to the silver level of responsibility. One of the best gifts you can give yourself and your dance partner is to improve your own dancing. That seems like a no-brainer—dancers want to improve their dancing!

> Personally, I am always ready to learn, although I do not always like being taught.
>
> *Winston Churchill*

Why, then, do we find ourselves resisting instruction? This is one of the weirdest experiences we have as we learn to dance. And we all do it, to a greater or lesser degree. It turns out that we humans all have a tendency to resist change.

> Human beings, who are almost unique
> in having the ability to learn from the
> experience of others, are also remarkable
> for their apparent disinclination to do so.
>
> *Douglas Adams*

Lessons and Coaching

Let's clarify what we mean when we talk about the teacher and the coach. Often we use the terms interchangeably. But there are times when you might receive instruction from a coach who is different from your regular teacher.

In many dance studios, especially those that have students or pros who compete, it is a common practice for coaches to be brought in from the outside. These coaches are usually judges at dance competitions; often former champions who have retired from competition. They stay for a day or two at a succession of studios, coaching students and pros alike. Everyone, not just students, can benefit from coaching. Sometimes coaches give group seminars, in addition to individual coaching.

Coaches may "tweak" existing choreography, create entire new routines, or spend time helping you polish a basic move you thought you already knew. Pierre Allaire told us he travelled all the way to England for a coaching session which turned out to be entirely about how to hold the lady's hand. He couldn't believe it—he had travelled all that way for that?! But, in hindsight, he feels it was the most valuable coaching he ever received.

Such coaching is expensive; normally the hourly rate is higher than private lessons with your regular teacher. (And you *should* be taking private lessons if you are serious about improving your dancing. You just can't get all the instructional attention you need in group classes.) With your teacher present, you have to pay your teacher's fee on top of the coaching fee.

It is best if your regular teacher is present during the coaching, as he or she has the bigger picture of your dance development and will be the one to follow up with you after the coach is gone. Sometimes, you are not ready for what the coach has to offer, and your teacher may make modifications in what the coach is asking you to do. For example, Art was quite wild when he first learned the tango. His technique was low, but his enthusiasm was high! When a visiting coach correctly began to smooth out some basic flaws, the teacher interceded. "I don't want him to lose his enthusiasm yet!"

Even if you don't compete, it is a great idea to take coaching when it is available. This is not because the coach has any secret information that your dance teacher doesn't have, but because the more different ways you hear something explained, and the more really good dancers you dance with, the more likely you are to have an "aha" experience when you will finally understand something that seemed opaque to you until that moment. (When this occurs, resist the temptation to say to your teacher, "How come *you* never told me that?" The coach and your teacher will both fall over laughing. *Of course* your teacher told you! You just never got it before! The coach's different way of explaining it suddenly made sense to you.)

Yes, dance lessons and coaching are expensive, but no dance expense brings a greater return for the investment than lessons and coaching from competent dance professionals. But here is the oddity: despite the expense, dancers waste many of these precious hours because they resist learning what is being taught. ("I didn't do that!" "That is exactly what I did!" "I'm already doing what you're telling me!" "You can't want me to do *that*!") Why do we all, at times, react like this?

Unrealistic Self Perception—A Good Thing in Moderation

You may remember that in Chapter 1 we talked about how dancing can assault our defenses. Our experience at our first private lesson is a good example. We thought we were much better dancers than we really were. Furthermore, it was useful for us to have this mistaken self-perception, this "positive illusion" (see Taylor, 1991, for more on positive illusions). It helped us get out and dance in public, and have fun while doing it, because we "knew" we were terrific. And it was not so wrong. (Though more wrong than we imagined.) For our level of training and experience, we were fine. But in order to get better, we needed more instruction, and in order to receive more instruction, we had to be able to take criticism. Here's what happened:

When we first took up dancing, we began by enrolling in group classes through our local community college. After a while, some friends convinced us that we should take private lessons from a teacher they had started working with. They were better dancers than we were, so we followed their advice.

Our new teacher interviewed us about what we wanted to learn.

"The bolero," we enthused.

"Do you know how to rumba?" she asked.

"No," we replied.

"Well, I think you should learn the rumba first," she said.

Of course she was right, but we were a little disappointed. Then she said she would like to see us do a dance we knew. We asked for a waltz, our best dance, and we waltzed our little hearts out. When she stopped the music, did we hear what we half expected? "Wow! That was wonderful! I can see we don't need to spend much time on the waltz!"

No, we did not. She said something like, "Hmm," or, "I see." No flowers, no compliments. Again, we were disappointed. We started to work.

In hindsight it is laughable that we thought she would burst into applause for our poor little waltz. We were beginning bronze students, with no idea of what we didn't know. But we were very pleased with ourselves. We could really get out on the dance floor and waltz in time to the music (mostly) without stepping on each other! We could move pretty easily around an empty floor! These were new skills for us. And it was fun. We were comparing ourselves to where we had started a year or so before. She saw us more realistically, through the eyes of a professional. She was probably thinking, "Where do I begin with these two?!"

> Every act of conscious learning requires the willingness to suffer an injury to one's self-esteem. That is why young children, before they are aware of their own self-importance, learn so easily.
>
> *Thomas Szasz*

Taking criticism means giving up a bit (or a lot!) of our inflated idea of how wonderful we are—an idea we keep trying to defend. But if we keep defending an exaggerated idea of our ability in order to maintain self-esteem, how can we ever learn? In fact, coaches tell us that this is a common problem. They try to give accurate and useful information to dancers who want to improve, yet students often react by arguing with them. So the coach has a very difficult job—giving criticism in such a way that it can be heard and used.

And the student faces two different types of hurdles in learning to benefit from dance instruction: the first is emotional, and the second is cognitive. Let's start by examining some of the emotional issues.

Emotional Issues

Pride and Shame

Coaches tell us that, in general, adults are harder to teach than children or college students. People who are still in school are used to being in the position of "learner," and accepting the authority of the teacher.

Adults taking dance lessons may be people who feel successful outside of dance. They may be justifiably proud of what they have achieved and may be used to being the "go to" person, the problem-solver, the sock-finder. If they are used to enjoying the positive illusion that they are always "right," or used to telling subordinates what to do, they may have more difficulty accepting the "one down" position that is required to acknowledge the superior knowledge of the teacher or coach. People who feel competent at home or at work sometimes forget that such expertise means nothing on the dance floor. If you are usually "right," it can be tough to accept being told you are "wrong" in dancing. And being told by someone half your age! This is one of the reasons why it is so important to have coaching from someone whose dance knowledge and skill you truly respect.

Whether you are a world-famous surgeon, or just an ordinary, reasonably competent adult, if you think your prior accomplishments will help you learn to dance well, you are in for a rude shock. But if you bring to your study of dance the persistence you brought to your previous learning, instead of dropping out, you will be able to tolerate lots of potentially embarrassing moments as you are told, over and over again, to move your body in ways you thought would be easy, but aren't.

> **Remember- Everything is simple. Nothing is easy.**
>
> *Ray Rivers*

Sometimes the feeling that other students are watching can add to feelings of shame or embarrassment since they see the mistakes we make during our lesson. We may feel that we lose face in their eyes. Art recalls feeling embarrassed as another student appeared to be watching him intently during a lesson. He became increasingly uncomfortable at having to dance the same section over and over again as the teacher tried to help him improve. "What a klutz I must look like," he thought. When the student approached him after the lesson, gushing with admiration over his dancing, he was amazed.

But isn't our feeling of embarrassment just a reflection of our inner attitude? Why is there any shame in being a student? Isn't learning the point of teaching? The student who will get the most from any teaching is the one who listens to whatever the coach says, tries to understand it fully, and applies it in practice.

> **Being ignorant is not so much a shame as being unwilling to learn.**
>
> *Benjamin Franklin*

In reality, we are neither as wonderful as we wish, nor as awful as we fear—in dancing, or in any other aspect of life (and not being that wonderful is *soooo* disappointing!). Pride and shame are two sides of the same coin. Learning to accept the ongoing criticism that is necessary for improvement in any sport, including dance, is a mental discipline that helps us become more mature adults.

Pay attention to your inner processes the next time you have a lesson. Watch as you revert to a six-year-old (hopefully only on the inside, where no one hears) when corrected. "It's not my fault!" "I certainly did exactly what you told me to do and now you're saying it's wrong? Make up your mind!" Yes, you're not the only one. We all have that brat inside.

It's not your fault? Who cares? It's irrelevant. Erase blame or fault as a response to correction. It's a waste of time, money, and learning. Gradually replace the automatic inner, "It's not my fault!" response with, "I'll get this eventually." Your dancing will improve faster, even though it's another receding horizon...

> When a man points a finger at someone else, he should remember that four of his fingers are pointing at himself.
>
> *Louis Nizer*

Once you cut back on defensiveness, but begin to explain why you made the error... Congratulations! You've progressed from six to fourteen! Sorry, you're still not at the adult level.

The "reasons why" may well be valid, but they are just as irrelevant. (Another %@#! growth experience!) To improve, try embracing problems and using the coach to help you learn how to deal with them, even if they are valid, external, and compelling.

Were you distracted because someone just walked in? Wonderful! Seize this as an opportunity to learn to focus better. Did your dance partner put weight on you? It would be better if this never happened, but what do I do if it does happen? Refrain from blaming your partner or yourself. Instead, ask your teacher how to solve the problem. Often the answer will surprise you.

Art recalls an early experience in which his teacher was trying to help him learn to focus better: I found I couldn't smile, much less dance, if my partner talked with me. So I was quite surprised when my teacher began to chat with me as we danced during a lesson. "How are your children?" "Did you have a good time on your vacation?" "Do you like Chinese food?" Each time, I stopped dancing to answer. Finally I said, a bit put out, "I can't dance if you keep talking to me!" "Yes, I know," she replied, "that's why I'm doing it!"

Cultivating Genuine Humility

Champions are sometimes known more for their arrogance than for their humility. But the true championship attitude is one of *genuine* humility—not self-abasement (which shows a lack of self-respect), but continuous openness to receiving feedback. That attitude shows confidence in the ability to keep improving.

> You can always become better.
>
> *Tiger Woods*

As children, we all experienced the feeling of being unjustly criticized by parents, teachers, or other children. So it is easy for us, now, to relive those old feelings when we are criticized, whether justifiably or not. And, depending on the reality of our adult lives, there may be times when it is important for us to defend ourselves in the face of criticism. Lack of defense in response to criticism may, in some circumstances, be taken as a sign of weakness. On the job a good defense may save you from being eaten by sharks.

The dance studio, on the other hand, should be a safe place to learn. This depends on having a respectful relationship with your teacher. As we pointed out in Chapter 2, you must respect the person instructing you. Equally, you need to feel respected by your teacher in order to experience a safe learning environment. Teachers must also be careful to show respect, not only to the student in front of them, but to all students. After all, if you hear your teacher ridiculing another student, you may well think, "When will it be my turn?"

In a safe learning environment, criticism is not personal; it is objectively focused on the dancing. When teachers and coaches model this attitude, it will gradually become more possible for students to stop personalizing dance feedback and become more objective about analyzing how they are using their bodies to convey the dance. (Teachers, for more on creating a positive learning experience for students, see *Some Basic Principles of Human Learning as Applied to Teaching Dance* at the end of this book.)

When we can move away from our old responses of automatic defense and open ourselves to really receive coaching, we take our learning to a new level. We can relax and have more fun. And, perhaps for the first time, we may begin to use the experience of learning as a kind of meditation, or Zen study.

> When the student is ready, the master appears.
>
> *Buddhist Proverb*

Cognitive and Perceptual Issues

My Brain Doesn't Know What My Body Is Doing!

Now let's shift from exploring some of the emotional obstacles to learning to thinking about cognitive roadblocks to learning to dance. For many of us, understanding instructions about moving our bodies is like those package inserts that tell you how to put a new appliance together in Chinese, Korean, and Turkish—but not English. It may be perfectly correct, but for me, it's incomprehensible!

If you have a background in sports, you are lucky. Dancing, after all, is a sport, as well as an art. If you have received coaching in another sport, you have a general idea of how to focus on what your body is doing, even though dance terminology is different. You also have experience in being given critical feedback by a coach.

For the rest of us, it is dismaying to discover that being "smart" is, basically, irrelevant.

Words are just woefully inadequate to convey what to do with our bodies; in fact, we may not even know where our bodies are in space. One of the most fascinating, unexpected benefits of learning to dance is developing a much greater awareness of body placement and use. (We firmly believe that the improved posture and balance that result from studying dance will not only prolong our lives, but will vastly enhance our quality of life as we age.)

Good coaches know how inadequate language is for conveying body feelings, which is why they don't just talk, they dance with you. They also use metaphors that they have found effective in their own careers to help them produce the desired body shapes and movement. (Here are a few we have heard: "Pretend you are turning a doorknob." "Imagine you have an expensive jewel in the hollow of your throat and you want everyone to see it." "Picture a hot cup of coffee on your shoulder." "Think of throwing yourself ten feet through a door." "Present your fruit on a silver platter.")

The reason we have difficulty connecting the words of instruction to the correct use of our bodies is that we process language in a different part of the brain from the part we use to control our movement through space. For most of us, the connections between these parts are weak. To demonstrate this, try this exercise for fun. You will probably be surprised at the outcome.

Skill Practice: Spatial Body Awareness

Looking straight ahead, stand with your feet twelve inches apart, toes parallel, facing forward. Line up your knees so they are straight. Now look down. Are your feet twelve inches apart? Are your feet and legs lined up as you thought, exactly parallel, or are they aligned differently?

Since we are typically unaware of what we are doing with our bodies in any detailed way, and since words do such a poor job of conveying this information, we must constantly seek clarification from our coaches. "Is this what you mean?" "What image do you use to get your body to do that?" "From what body part are you starting that motion?" "What do you mean by 'forward'? Down the line of dance, toward my partner, or in the direction my hips are facing?"

> When you know something, say what you know. When you don't know something, say that you don't know. That is knowledge.
>
> *Confucius*

Ask and try, try and ask, ask and try. When your teacher finally says, "Yes, that's it!" pay attention to how your body felt when you "got it." What image did you use to get it? Encoding the feeling and the words in the thinking part of your brain can sometimes help you capture the bodily sensation so that you can re-create it when you need it.

But do not fear that you may not be able to re-create the feeling. You won't. Not at first. Don't be surprised if you are not even sure what you did! But here's the weird part: if you over-focus on your anxiety about not knowing or not understanding, that will actually interfere with your learning. In this mode of learning, you have to simply allow it to wash over you and trust that if you keep at it you will eventually get the movement consistently.

> When you cannot see what is happening, do not stare harder. Relax and look gently with your inner eye.
>
> *Lao Tzu*

As you focus more and more on where your body is and how you are using it, you will have the opportunity to make many interesting discoveries about yourself. Art, for example, discovered that he did not think of himself as having feet—just stumps! What a shock! No wonder he had so much difficulty in rolling through his feet—he had no perception of having feet. This likely stemmed from years of having bunions and poorly fitted shoes—he had simply blocked out awareness of his feet, an adaptive coping mechanism earlier in life, but maladaptive for dancing now.

Betty discovered that she had fear associated with the use of her left arm, left over from a dislocated elbow at the age of four. Once she realized the source of her fear, she could begin to let it go.

The Words Get in the Way

It is not only that words are inadequate to convey body sensations; they almost seem to add to the confusion. We bring with us to the task of learning to dance the same strategies for learning that have worked for us in other situations, verbal strategies. But much of what is taught doesn't seem to make sense at first. So when the teacher says, "Keep your head back," we automatically think, "Well she really doesn't mean *that* far back, because that feels too odd, so she must mean just straight up." This "inner translation" is so instantaneous, initially, that we do not even realize we are doing it. Only over time, as we gradually get feedback about how it feels when we think it is wrong, but it is really correct, and vice versa, do we begin to let go of our preconceived ideas and develop an inner vocabulary that works for us.

Betty recalls: Keeping my head back, in what is a correct position for dancing, felt very hard to do at first not because it was physically difficult, but because it felt too haughty. It just felt like a conflict with my personality to be in a body posture that felt supercilious. I had to get over the feeling that it was kind of "mean" to have that "haughty" head position before I could produce it with any consistency.

Art adds: I am still working on the concept of keeping my "hips forward." Such a position feels like it goes against everything I was taught to avoid sexually harassing women. Of course, it really isn't sexual in dancing; it just feels so wrong.

We have the experience over and over again of complaining that a certain body movement feels "weird" only to be told, "Good, that means you are getting it. It does feel weird at first." Or, even odder, "You are having pain there? Terrific! That is just the place that ought to hurt. Good for you. It means you're using the correct muscle now!"

"In the early stages of our partnership," Betty recalls, "my teacher, Louis Soma, had to be rather strict with me to get me to stop overusing the verbal part of my brain. For two whole years he told me, 'Don't think, just feel!' It was scary! I had no idea of how to learn just with my body. I felt like I was jumping off a cliff without a parachute, which demanded a high level of courage and trust. Finally, when I could begin to let go of solving my dance problems 'logically,' he said, 'OK, now you can add thinking back in.'"

Dancing Is a Perceptual Illusion

The more experienced you become as a dancer, the more you understand that dancing is like a magician's illusion—smoke, mirrors, and misdirection. When the man looks like he's holding the woman up, she's actually holding herself up. When it looks like he is throwing her in a tango—he isn't. She's moving herself. Need more space to dance? Move *closer* to your partner, not farther away—but with the correct body part. But until you have learned all this you have to take it on faith, which is another reason to work only with teachers and coaches whose expertise you respect. So have patience, and enjoy your present moment.

Take Responsibility for Practicing

> Knowing is not enough; we must apply. Willing is not enough; we must do.
>
> *Johann von Goethe*

Practice is one of the few things in life that cannot be successfully delegated. The only way to get better at anything is to do it over and over. But repeating any action incorrectly only serves to perpetuate and strengthen error. So, to be useful, practice must be done with the best mental attitude and physical technique we can muster at that moment. At the same time, we must accept that at a later stage we may have to unlearn some of what we learned earlier in order to move to a higher level. This is the natural process of development. If you can accept this, you will not lose heart when it happens. (Or you won't lose as much heart...)

> Do what you can, with what you have, and where you are.
>
> *Dan Millman*

In Chapter 6 we focused on how to have a successful dance practice session with a partner. Here we are focusing on your individual responsibility for practice. At a silver level of responsibility you cannot wait for your partner to be ready, for the floor to be available, or for a myriad of other obstacles that crop up in real life to prevent you from practicing with your partner on a dance floor. At the silver level, if you want to improve you must take active charge of your own learning. The good news is that regardless of your life circumstances, you really *can* practice *something* every day, if you want to. Here are some examples of dance skills you can practice as you move through your daily life:

Practicing While Walking: Moving with a lifted torso; rolling through your feet; allowing the moving leg to swing; smiling; lining up your head over your spine; looking straight ahead and a little bit up; breathing with conscious awareness.

Practicing While Driving: Toning abdominal muscles; straightening your spine, lifting your torso up out of your waist; pulling your shoulder blades down; smiling; breathing with conscious awareness; identifying the beat of songs on the radio and deciding what dance you could do to the music (all while keeping your eyes on the road).

Practicing While in a Meeting: Rotating and flexing your ankles under the table; toning abdominal muscles; straightening your spine, lifting your torso up out of your waist; pulling your shoulder blades down. (Good posture can be practiced even if you are chairing the meeting!).

Practicing While Waiting for the Elevator: Patience; positive attitude; smiling; posture; balance; and, while you're at it, take the stairs for some work on your stamina!

Practicing at Home: Standing on one foot at a time to improve balance (you can do this while talking on the phone); practicing your heels and toes or other small sections of footwork; practicing posture, sway, and arm positions in front of a mirror; smiling; and breathing with conscious awareness.

Mental Practice: In addition to physical practice, there are also many opportunities for daily mental practice. This is particularly useful when you are learning a new routine. You can use otherwise "wasted" time by running a routine in your head when you are waiting for an appointment. As you picture each movement, picture the "coaching" that goes with it (for example, "Keep your left side up!" "Compress!" or, counting a syncopation, "1–2 *and* 3."). If you get to a "stuck" place where you can't picture what comes next, this tells you that you have not yet learned that part of the routine. Make a note of this, and take it to your next lesson so you can be sure to work on it with your teacher.

> I am always doing that which I cannot do, in order that I may learn how to do it.
>
> *Pablo Picasso*

Enjoying Practice

You will get the most benefit from practicing with a positive mental attitude. We all have times when we just want to sit and read a book or relax in a hot tub. Accept that, and do what you enjoy. You will feel better and be able to bring a better attitude to your practice if you do not beat yourself up over it. But when you do decide to practice, smile and decide that you're going to have a good time.

Practicing small segments is another way to feel good about practice. If you stand on one foot and rotate your ankles ten times in each direction every day when you get up, it will take you less than two minutes. You will improve over time, and you will feel good that you have practiced something that day that will contribute to your dancing. If you remember to stand up straight, breathe, and smile at some later point in the day, then you will have done two practices in one day. Wonderful! Whatever you can do will contribute to your development. Pat yourself on the back and give yourself credit for what you can do, rather than focusing on all the things you don't have time for, or have not yet learned to do. Over time, you will be surprised to see how even small segments of ongoing practice lead to visible improvement.

Remember what we said in Chapter 1 about perfectionism. High achievers are often perfectionists. Some amount of perfectionism can have a positive effect if it leads to a willingness to try repeatedly. But if it leads to unrealistic expectations, with anger, depression, or withdrawal in the face of mistakes, it is not helpful. Better than perfectionism is persistence; the willingness to try and try again, with the assurance that if you just show up and try, you cannot avoid improving.

> Great works are performed not by speed or strength but perseverance.
>
> **Samuel Johnson**

Review of Silver Level Responsibility: Active Learning

Why do we resist coaching?

* Taking criticism means giving up unrealistic self perceptions.
* We are used to being competent adults and we feel embarrassed.
* When we feel embarrassed, our "inner six-year-old" takes over.

Dancing can help us grow up and take responsibility for:

* Deleting blame from our inner operating systems
* Learning not to make excuses
* Cultivating genuine humility
* Learning to receive criticism as informational, not personal

My brain doesn't know what my body is doing

* Words are inadequate for conveying body information.
* Being "smart" is irrelevant.
* Dancing can help us:
  * Increase body awareness
  * Cultivate and trust a new way of learning
  * Understand and create perceptual illusions

Take responsibility for practicing:

* While walking
* While driving
* In meetings
* Waiting for the elevator
* At home
* Mental practice

Chapter 9

SILVER LEVEL RESPONSIVENESS: POWER ISSUES IN THE PARTNERSHIP

At the silver level of relationship fitness we are dealing with somewhat taboo subjects—sex and power. In Chapter 7 we discussed dancing and romancing, and in this chapter we will take up the even more taboo topic of power in relationships.

Individual Power

What has power got to do with dancing? The connection may not be obvious at first. We think of dancing as lyrical, romantic, beautiful—but, wait! Do you ever have the opportunity to watch high-level dancers move? Whether the dance style is ballroom, ballet, jazz, or tap—excellent dancers exude physical energy. And that energy is powerful. Watch really fine dancers; then watch ordinary couples at a social dance. It isn't the fancy moves that distinguish the high-level dancers but how they carry themselves, even in the way they walk onto the floor or take a bow. They exude energy or "electricity" in their bodies as they move. They move with power.

Dancing is movement. The dancer cannot move without energy to power that movement. At higher levels of dance, accessing and controlling power becomes increasingly important. Like other athletes and performers, dancers must find a way to use their inner power to achieve peak performances. Dance practice and fitness training can increase physical power. Mental training can increase emotional energy and feelings of confidence and competence. And even beginners who understand that showing power is good have a tremendous edge in looking better than they are.

> Mastering yourself is true power.
>
> *Lao-tzu*

You Brute!

But power can also mean power "over" someone. As the individuals in the dance partnership increase their own power, they must learn how to control and balance their use of power within the partnership. Most men have a tendency (and in the beginning they are often taught) to overuse their upper bodies in dancing, where men are generally stronger than women. This leads to common errors of "breaking the frame," so that the woman feels "pushed." If a woman is feeling physically overpowered, she may react with anger, much to her partner's surprise. The lady's, "You brute!" response is an all-too-common experience in partnered dancing.

From a lady's point of view, allowing her partner to push her while he is trying to learn correct body use can feel like she is letting herself be abused. Yet constant criticism won't help the gentleman learn more quickly. This is the point at which many partnerships break down. It is not only that women are not willing to put up with being physically harmed (nor should they); it is that the psychological feeling of being imposed upon in a physical way is so strong that it is hard for them to believe the man could be oblivious to it. (Art says: I was very surprised to learn that trying to turn Louis incorrectly—that is, with improper technique—actually hurt him.)

> Power can be seen as power with rather than power over, and it can be used for competence and co-operation, rather than dominance and control.
>
> *Anne L. Barstow*

When the man believes he has communicated the lead as clearly as he can, he may feel that the partner who doesn't follow is simply being passive aggressive. In moments of unpleasant physical contact, it is very hard to refrain from saying mean things to one's partner ("Bully!" "Bitch!"). But giving in to this impulse, with a resulting all-out blowup, can cause relationship damage that is difficult to repair (remember respect?). At this point, many couples decide, "I'd rather stay married than continue learning to dance."

Use Your Coach

Work closely with a good coach on power issues. Good coaches have the perspective of having helped many couples learn to develop their individual power and use it effectively without imposing it on their dance partner in a negative way. There are many ways a good coach can help. First, your coach can help by "normalizing" the situation—reassuring you that you are not the only couple that has had this trouble. Second, your coach can help you understand your partner's perspective. Since your coach knows how to dance both the man's and woman's part, your coach can help you understand the issues your partner is facing in a particular figure. For example, "If the lady does not have her head strongly to the left, the man will be unable to get around." Or, "The man must curve his foot inward as he steps back, or his partner will feel blocked." This can be very surprising because many times we are talking about a difference of just a few inches, something almost impossible to discover on your own.

Finally, since your coach will dance with both of you, you can each get individual feedback on the particular issues you need to address to improve your technique. If you value harmony in your relationship, when you listen to the criticism being directed toward your partner, this would be a really good time to resist the temptation to say, "Nah-nyah-nyah-nyah-nyah!" (Remember, you are on the same team.) Only moments later you will hear what you are doing wrong! The answer to the physical power struggle is always to learn better technique (in other words, learning those things for which *you* can take responsibility), but until the next level of technique is mastered, both members of the couple must learn to be patient with each other and believe their partner is trying to do his or her best.

As we noted in Chapter 4, the two members of the couple are likely to be at different levels of development in different areas. While the man was working on floor craft, for example, his partner was free to spend her time working on her posture. So she may be ahead of him in terms of posture. But it would be a mistake for her to feel smug. Her turn to be behind in dance development will come when she finds, to her shock, that she has to learn those alignments that were originally presented as his responsibility. The man and the woman need to cover the same issues, eventually, but not in the same order; however, no one tells you this in the beginning...

Furthermore, every issue you cover in learning to dance will be repeated. There is no such thing as being finished with fundamentals (remember the receding horizon?). We were reminded of this, once again, when we were surprised to hear a coach covering, with a beginning bronze student, exactly the same issue we were working on during our gold/advanced lesson.

Just as we always return to fundamentals of technique as we progress in our dance development, we must constantly return to the basics of respect and responsibility in our relationship development. Respect yourself and your partner and take responsibility for learning and dancing your own part. Then you will be ready to be responsive to the level of your ability at your particular level of dance development.

Awareness Leads to Responsiveness

As we discussed in Chapter 4, the challenge for both members of the couple is to become more aware—both of our own bodies, and of each other. Mutual attunement is not easy, but in those moments when it happens, it can be an amazing experience. It is more likely to occur if you have a regular partner you dance with all the time. Betty can now feel Art thinking of leading something and then changing his mind, all within a nanosecond. "How is it possible," you ask, "to feel what someone else is thinking?"

> ...for any image of movement there is a subtle, corresponding muscular impulse.
>
> *Dan Millman*

Probably it is because there are small shifts in the man's body which, through training, the woman has learned to feel so that she can be prepared to respond to them almost instantly (that is, within the time frame of the music). Because women are taught from the beginning that they must learn to pay attention to the small physical changes that constitute the "lead," they are generally ahead of their partners in the area of physical attunement within the partnership. Ladies need this skill to dance with different partners, as each gentleman feels a bit different. A good female dancer learns to ignore what, from her point of view, is "static"—extraneous movements the gentleman makes that do not provide her with any information about the "lead."

> Who is strong? One who governs his passions.
>
> *Pirkei Avot*

The Powerful Lady

When a woman puts weight on her partner it is not an expression of power; it is a failure to take responsibility. If she is putting weight on her gentleman, she is not standing up and staying on her own side (see Chapter 3). Art vividly recalls a 90-pound "little old lady" who leaned on him all through a social waltz. He was amazed at how exhausted he felt holding her up for just one dance!

Given the physical size and strength differences in the typical dance partnership, most women could not express power through brute force, even if they wanted to. Rather, the powerful lady is one who moves her own body in a strong and direct manner with balance and mental clarity about where she plans to go and how she is going to get there. This lady's power comes from good technique, particularly her control of energy through her feet, ankles, and hips, and her body shaping.

When the lady learns to achieve this kind of power, her partner ought to be delighted. A woman who moves herself with power makes her partner's job easier. He indicates the lead with a compression and a shape, and off she goes. He does not have to push or pull her anywhere. Freedom—he gets to dance!

> Water is fluid, soft, and yielding. But water will wear away rock, which is rigid and cannot yield. As a rule, whatever is fluid, soft, and yielding will overcome whatever is rigid and hard. This is another paradox: what is soft is strong.
>
> *Lao-Tzu*

But for some men there may be another dimension of experience as their partner becomes more powerful. If the partners are in a social relationship in which the man has had more power in the relationship, he may experience her newfound dance power as his loss. Until he realizes that having a powerful partner is like trading in his old sedan for a new sports car, he may find himself unaccountably angry, intimidated, or depressed.

And to further complicate matters, the powerful lady is generally pickier. She doesn't want her balance disturbed. She objects more strongly to errors of technique because she understands better how they interfere with her dancing. Although a loving partner may understand and even applaud this, he may still find it galling without knowing why. Another growth experience (sigh).

Disturbing the Status Quo

It is a truism of biology that all organisms tend toward homeostasis, that is, equilibrium. This is also true in relationships.

Once a couple has achieved a relationship that is comfortable enough for them that they want to stay in it, both members will tend to resist change. Learning to dance challenges the comfort zone of a relationship by introducing change. It is not possible to change only on the dance floor—any changes made there will ripple into the life of the couple, just as their couple issues off the floor affect their dancing.

The changes that occur in the couple relationship because of dancing are subtle. Thus, they are often outside of the awareness of both partners. All they may feel is a discomfort—a sense of danger, even. When you are changing you feel off balance, disorganized, disrupted. Some of the changes have to do with shifts in power within the couple relationship. Remember Chapter 4? The man is "in charge," in the higher power position, because he has the right to "lead." The woman is "in charge," in the higher power position, because, "She's the picture, he's the frame." But, wait—which of these is true? The answer is, they are both true. And they are both false. To be effective on the dance floor, the partners must achieve genuine teamwork in which power is generously and seamlessly shared.

If you don't believe this, watch championship-level dancing, either at a competition or on television. No matter what the style of dance, you should see two powerful people dancing as a team, so attuned and responsive to each other that there is no apparent "lead," just seemingly "effortless" teamwork. They make it look easy—a magical illusion achieved only through countless hours of work.

Partners or Siblings?

Think back to your childhood. Who had power in your family? In the typical family, adults have most of the power because they set the rules and control the resources. But children have desires, too, and they try to fulfill them as best they can within the power structure of their family.

How did you use your power as a child? One way might have been by pleasing those powerful adults. But another way could have been by refusing to cooperate with what the adults wanted. ("You can't make me!") The same is true in peer relationships—one can achieve interpersonal power by positive means (for example, by being helpful or developing valued skills, such as being good at sports) or by negative means, such as making fun of people, blaming others, or setting them up to look bad. Both positive and negative means are used by everyone to a greater or lesser degree, especially with siblings, our first rivals for parental love and attention.

The interpersonal skills we develop with our siblings become strong habits. Hopefully, most of us grow out of the negative aspects of these habits as we mature, but under stress we all revert to more primitive versions of ourselves. In the dance partnership, stress may bring out the worst in sibling-like rivalry, where you treat your partner as a rival for approval. And the descent into sibling-like rivalry may happen so quickly that we are totally unprepared for the feeling.

It doesn't make mature sense, but under stress, the child-part of our brain may feel like this is a zero-sum game, where if one gets more, the other gets less, rather than remembering that partnered dancing is a team sport. The reality is: "If I look good, you look good. If you are a mess, it won't help me."

But time and again, we have seen couples who express rivalry within the partnership. There was the woman who told the coach: "You fix him, then I'll dance with him," as she contemptuously left the dance floor. She was referring to her own husband! Clearly she conveyed that she considered herself to be a far superior dancer, whose husband was beneath her. Expressing such an attitude could not have been good for their marriage, but if she was expressing it on the dance floor, could that be the only place she was expressing it?

Ballroom dancing is a couple activity. Without partnership it cannot exist at all. To be a ballroom dancer is to be in a symbiotic relationship. Although both members of the couple need and must depend on each other, it is common for each to secretly feel that they could do better, if only their partner would shape up. Knowing you need your partner while, at the same time, feeling that your partner is keeping you from achieving greatness, can produce high levels of frustration that can erupt into rage and, ultimately, result in the dissolution of the partnership. But in a dance partnership, as in a marriage, partners are in the same boat. And if I chop a hole in "your" side of the boat to spite you, get back at you, or make you look bad, "my" side won't float. I am not just hurting you, I am hurting myself—we will go down together.

For the partnership to work well, both members of the couple must find ways to express their power that enhance, rather than interfere with, the couple relationship. And that same quest—to find ways to channel and share the power we develop individually—will also feed the power of the dance couple as a team. The more we can "draft" off each other (like race cars in the slip stream of the car ahead), the more power we will have with less feeling of struggle.

If you find yourself treating your partner as a sibling you have to outcompete, you need to back off and take a serious look at your relationship. People who care about and respect their partners want to support them to improve, and learn to cover for their errors. It's not about showing everyone that you are better as an individual, it's about making the team look better. Great dancing projects respect, responsibility, and responsiveness.

Good dancers are not intimidated by their partner's power, they are energized by it. He stimulates her, she responds, thereby sparking a reaction from him, propelling the action forward into the next cycle. They appear balanced, centers moving toward each other, shifting and changing as one, powerful in their unity. And, although dancing with a powerful lady can feel intimidating at first, Art can attest that you can learn to match it, and be thrilled by it.

> I do not try to dance better than anyone else. I only try to dance better than myself.
>
> *Mikhail Baryshnikov*

Finding the Center

To achieve shared power, we must first develop individual power; then learn how to share it. Learning to find our own balance and locate our own "center" opens the path to developing power. Dancers talk a lot about the "center." Each dancer has his or her own center. The feeling of being centered is a feeling of balance among all aspects of the self. When you are centered, the physical, mental/emotional, and spiritual forces within you are aligned. You are balanced over your feet and around your spine. You can breathe and move with controlled energy. As you learn to develop this feeling, you will increasingly be able to access it and experience it as a physical sensation, one that is both peaceful and powerful.

Exercise: Finding Your Center

To locate your individual center, stand with erect, but relaxed posture, with your hands at your sides. Align your spine and hold up your head. Breathe deeply, but naturally. As you exhale, allow yourself to be aware of feeling your breath release from deep inside your belly. This is your center. Most people experience it about two inches below the belly button, although it can move.

Once you have located your center, make a practice of being more aware of it. Your center is a power source for your dancing. Gaining mental control of your center will give you more physical and mental control of your body, improve your balance and help you feel grounded to the floor. Your center is the place where your inner power is concentrated.

Don't give up hope if you are having difficulty finding your center. Most people do not find it "once and for all." At best, they find it, then lose it, then find it again. It is a lifelong quest. With practice over time, however, you will be able to access this power source more quickly and easily, use it more effectively, and stay connected to it for longer periods of time. If you are interested in more work on the center, you may want to study Tai Chi, one of the martial arts, or Pilates.

The couple also has a center. When both members of the dance partnership learn to find and use their centers, they can share power between them, passing it back and forth and working off each other through their shared center. They are mutually attuned and responsive. Responsiveness through a powerful center produces a positive experience for both members of the couple. The truth is, one member of the dance couple cannot move unless the other is doing the reciprocal.

He vacates space, she fills it. He begins a line, and she finishes it. He goes, she goes. Action and reaction. Each person does only their own half of the dance, and trusts their partner to do the other half.

Couples who have learned how to share their power move with fluidity. They make it look easy. They are the ones you can't help but admire, even if you don't know why. But sharing power is a high-level achievement. In dancing, as in so many areas of life, it is easier said than accomplished.

> The most powerful weapon on earth is the human soul on fire.
>
> *Ferdinand Foch*

Review of Silver Level Responsiveness: Power Issues in the Partnership

Good dancers learn to develop and use power

Power within the partnership must be balanced and controlled
* Too much upper body power can feel abusive to the lady.
* Awareness leads to mutual responsiveness.
* Some men may need help to appreciate a powerful woman.

Your partner is your team-mate, not your rival

Find your center and learn to connect to your partner's center

Chapter 10

APPLYING RELATIONSHIP SKILLS IN PERFORMANCE AND COMPETITION

Not every dancer competes, but most dancers engage in performances of some type, whether a "showcase," (studio dance recital) once or twice a year, or a "bar contest." Even students who only dance socially often discover the extent to which others watch them. Anyone who takes lessons has had the experience of having their dancing commented on favorably by the band leader, the maitre d', or onlookers at social events. To the extent that others watch you, you *are* performing—so don't fight it, accept it! And when you notice others watching you, you will pull your head and shoulders back, and try to dance a bit better, which is a good thing.

> Dance is music made visible.
>
> **George Balanchine**

Performing and competing can be valuable aids to a dancer's development by providing a deadline and specific goals that help to focus lessons and practice. The downside is that performance anxiety or an over-focus on "winning" may interfere with learning and enjoyment, which can stress the partnership.

When we feel anxiety we easily slip into old habits of blame. ("If only my partner were a better dancer I would look *so* good!" "I got this already, why doesn't he?") So when we are preparing to perform, we must maintain a heightened level of vigilant care for each other and for our partnership. Here, more than ever, we can depend on our old friends, the **3 Rs** of Relationship Fitness, to help us stay calm and focused on our mutual goal, no matter what may happen in the heat of the moment.

Respect

Respect Yourself

The first step, as always, is to respect *yourself*. When you prepare for any performance, you will be doing a lot of practice to make sure that the performance is as good as you can make it at your level of skill. At the same time, we can always find details in any performance we wish we had done better. But an important difference between practicing and performing is that when it is time to perform, we must shift gears and put all the focus on details and self-critique aside. Performance time is the time to go out and *sell* to the audience grace, energy, and joy. So when you walk out on the floor, even before the music starts, your performance has begun. Stand up and smile! Project that self-respect!

If the choreography goes off track, keep smiling and tune in to your partner so you can agree (nonverbally) on how to get back on track. Keep in mind that no one but your partner and your coach know what your choreography is supposed to be, anyway, so if you do something that was unplanned, have fun and make it look good!

> Dance first. Think later. It's the natural order.
>
> *Samuel Beckett*

Respect Your Partner

Performance tests partnership. You must trust each other to work together as a team, and commit to doing whatever it takes to make each other look good. When inevitably, mistakes happen, you cover for each other. When things go well, you cheer for each other; whatever happens, keep a sense of perspective and your sense of humor. Remember, how many couples even have the courage to dance, let alone compete?

The first time we competed, we danced three dances: Intermediate Bronze waltz, tango, and fox trot in the American style. It was a small, local competition, but both of us were very nervous. When we went out onto the floor, Art led the fox trot routine to the waltz music. At that level in the American style, the patterns are pretty interchangeable, and Art danced in time to the music, so Betty could follow. When he got to the fox trot, Art thought, "Didn't I already dance this? It feels so familiar..." By the time he figured out that he had danced his fox trot routine twice, the music was over, and we went off the floor, laughing to ourselves. A stranger standing near the on-deck area said to us, "Either you two are great actors, or you were having a heckuva good time out there!" We very much appreciated this compliment from a total stranger. This stranger later became our dance teacher, Louis Soma.

> Common sense and a sense of humor are the same thing, moving at different speeds. A sense of humor is just common sense, dancing.
>
> *Clive James*

We weren't great dancers by any means, but we were having fun, and that is fun to watch. Think about dancers you have watched, perhaps on the show, "Dancing with the Stars." It is common, especially in the early rounds, for the stars that are fun to watch to get the most votes, even if they are not the best dancers. And even at higher levels of skill, the person who projects an attitude of having a great time in the dance and caring toward their partner is more enjoyable to watch than someone with perfect footwork who performs their routine like a robot.

When we were first learning to dance, we attended a showcase at another dance studio. A high-level amateur couple who had spent many years on their technique danced one of the numbers. But they didn't look like they were having any fun. At the end of their dance, they obviously disagreed about which direction they were going to take when they walked off the floor after their bow. They ended up exiting in different directions, and it was evident to the onlookers that this was not planned—they were having a spat during a performance! This public dispute undermined all the hard work they had put into preparing their performance. And the memory of their shocking display continued to affect our attitude toward them when we saw them performing at other venues.

The moral is: if you and your dance partner are having a tough time getting along, have the self-control to keep that under wraps in public situations. When you are in a public venue your audience, and the judges (if it is a competition) also see you in the hallway, in the restaurant, or checking into the hotel—not just on the dance floor. Displays of disrespect in the partnership that they might see in these informal situations cannot help but color the way they look at you when you perform.

Respect the Organizers and Judges

Running a dance competition is a hugely complex undertaking. (A studio showcase, though much smaller, is complex, too.) There are so many details to keep track of. There can be problems with the floor, the sound system, and the room temperature. The caterers may have servers quit, and the computers, on which we have become so dependent for scheduling and scoring, may suddenly get stage fright and unaccountably freeze up. There are always last-minute entries and last-minute changes. People get sick or simply don't show up. Planes are late and luggage is lost. Yet the show must somehow go on.

In the midst of it all, a successful organizer appears calm and welcoming. He/she is so happy you came. S/he hopes you like the food, your seats in the ballroom, and the show. (The master of this art, Sam Sodano, the owner of the Ohio Star Ball, is the most successful competition organizer in the United States.)

No matter how important you are, you are a small cog in this enterprise. The organizers and their staff are doing the best they can to put on a successful event. If there is a problem, of course you should bring it to the attention of the appropriate person, but, please, do it respectfully. Your basic attitude should be, "I'm sorry to bother you, but I know you would want to help me..." rather than, "I'm very annoyed that I am being inconvenienced."

If you have never been to a dance competition you should go, both because it is fun to watch, and because you will learn something. While you are there, watch the judges. These people are working hard. They are on their feet many hours a day with few breaks. They have, in general, 90 seconds to look at a field of dancers and make a quick decision about placements. Try it yourself. It's hard to do, especially if the couples are closely matched! Sometimes you see in a later dance someone whose dancing you didn't notice earlier. Should you have placed them higher two dances ago? You didn't see them on the other side of the ballroom. Never mind, there is no time for regrets, because here comes the next heat.

Yes, the judges deserve our respect, no matter how they place us. If you don't get the marks you hoped for, don't get mad at the judges; they're just doing their job. They have to mark what they see, no matter how much they might like you personally. So just go back to the studio and work harder. If you keep at it, you'll do better the next time.

Respect Other Dancers

What is being judged at a competition? Some judge the top line (head and frame), some judge the feet, some judge movement across the floor, and everyone judges posture and partnership. But good sportsmanship is another factor that can affect judging, so even if you're not Miss (or Mr.) America, you can try to be Miss (or Mr.) Congeniality. This doesn't mean you should back off in your dancing and yield space to others. You still have to be physically aggressive to look good, but you don't have to be interpersonally aggressive. By all means, take your space, but don't knock over another couple to do it!

Remember your ballroom manners. Try to avoid colliding with other dancers. If there is a collision, pause briefly to make sure everyone is all right, then continue. When you are off the floor you can then seek out the person you inadvertently kicked or elbowed to further apologize.

Other competitors are your colleagues, not your enemies. Most of them are very nice people, whom it is fun to get to know.

Another time, you will be glad you were nice to them when they help you out by lending you their shoe brush, pinning on your number, or telling you your strap is showing.

> It is not true that nice guys finish last; nice guys are winners before the game even starts.
>
> *Addison Walker*

Though studio showcases are like mini-competitions in some ways, you generally have the floor to yourself, unless you are in a formation. Even so, you will probably have to share dressing room space, and you will surely have to stand in line at some point, whether at the buffet or to enter the ballroom. Keep in mind that everyone else is at least as nervous as you are, and that, under pressure, people tend to revert to their child-selves. If need be, try to be the only grown-up in the room—not by bossing people around or giving unasked-for advice, but by being calm and mature, waiting for your turn, and being kind and compassionate toward yourself, your partner, and everyone else.

Respect the Activity

Treating all the people involved respectfully is an important way to show respect for a dance showcase or competition. Another way is to follow the rules. This sounds so obvious that you wouldn't think any adult would need to be told to do it. Unfortunately, many people think "the rules" (any rules!) don't apply to them (because they are "special," they know the organizers, or whatever). If you rate "special" status, one of the best ways to show this is by following the rules.

The rules for competition are commonly available on the websites of the sponsoring organizations, as well as in the programs available on site. Read and follow them. In general, they will tell you how you are expected to dress, when you should be in the ballroom (generally half an hour before your scheduled heat time), whether you are allowed to photograph or video the dancing, and what material you are allowed to dance at the level you have entered. If you are unsure about any of these things, this would be a great topic of conversation with your teacher or coach. At a competition, you represent your teacher, as well as yourself, so your teacher has a definite interest in having you not only dance well, but behave appropriately, too.

At a studio dance showcase, you may not have posted rules but you will have been told by the organizers what they expect you to do. They will need you to come to required rehearsals, be at the venue at a specified time, and be groomed and ready to go on several numbers ahead of when you are dancing.

When you are a member of the audience, please be enthusiastic—yell and cheer all you want to—that is part of the fun. At dance competitions the dancers appreciate having you call out their numbers to cheer them on. But don't take other people's seats or stand up in the front so others can't see. Finally, at the risk of sounding terribly old-fashioned, please don't show up in torn jeans and an old sweatshirt. Dressing like ladies and gentlemen in the ballroom is an important way for spectators to show their respect for the activity.

Responsibility

Practice

Your biggest responsibility is your individual preparation. In addition to working on your technique, which you are always doing, you must learn the choreography that you will be performing. And the best way to learn choreography is to practice.

> One must do the same subject over again ten times, a hundred times. Nothing in art must seem an accident, not even movement.
>
> *Edgar Degas*

You can practice with your partner and you can practice by yourself. It is more difficult to practice alone because you cannot dance "full out" by yourself—you don't have your partner's energy to respond to—but you can at least "walk through" the choreography by yourself. This can be especially useful to the man in helping him identify those points where the choreography seems murky, since he is supposed to be "leading;" but it is important for the lady, too, especially at higher levels where the choreography becomes more complex and demanding and both partners share the lead.

You can always practice choreography mentally. Can you run the routine in your mind? If there is a point in the mental run-through where your inner tape stops, you can be sure it will be unclear when you dance it. This is a great way to prepare for a lesson. Run the routine in your mind, and if you hit a point where you feel unsure, note it so you can clarify the issue with your teacher.

Don't believe that you must have a standard-sized ballroom and a partner to practice. You can practice your posture wherever you go. And you can practice little bits of a routine in the kitchen of your own apartment. Pick out something that needs work but not a lot of floor space (heel turns? a sailor shuffle?). Practice these bits of choreography in a small space. It *will* make a difference.

> ...a little of something is much better than a lot of nothing...
>
> *Dan Millman*

Physical Preparation

In Chapter 5 we told you that competing made us realize we had to do more to prepare our bodies to dance. If you are getting ready to compete or perform, this would be a good time to review the advice in Chapter 5 about taking care of your body. Wanting to look good on the dance floor just might give you the motivation you need to do what you ought to be doing anyway for long-term good health.

But whether you begin to make positive lifestyle changes or not, you will still need to do extra preparation to care for your body during a competition. There are no breaks for lunch at large competitions, so you might have to dance through lunch. Normally, you will not be able to find this out ahead of time.

When you arrive at the venue, get your program. Look for program inserts with changes. Detailed schedules are not made available until just before the competition to allow for late entries. The organizers do not know how much time they need to allow for each event until they know how many entries they have. Unfortunately, many dancers do not submit entries until the very last moment.

Bottom line: plan to have snacks that work for you. Take what you need. Snacks for the ballroom should give you enough energy that you don't "hit a wall" with an energy drop, but should be light enough that you don't feel too full. (That full feeling makes you feel like napping, not dancing.) Avoid messy foods that might spill onto your costume or give you sticky fingers. Bananas, nuts, and yogurt are generally good snacks. Lots of dancers like energy bars, but try them out in advance—some of them taste terrible! Take your own sports drink. Water is generally available in the ballroom.

If you are performing in an unfamiliar venue, don't count on *anything* to be provided. Take whatever you might need. If you are prepared to be self-sufficient you will feel more relaxed and calm. This will help you and your partner.

Remember to hydrate before competing or performing. Begin drinking extra water the day before and continue on the day of the performance. Ladies have a special issue with hydration. Most ladies' dance costumes have sewed-in dance pants; to use the restroom means disrobing and dropping your gown on the floor of the stall. So buy a gown that is easy to get in and out of; and plan trips to the restroom when you have enough time between heats, whether you think you need to go or not. If you wait until you have to go, it might be when you need to dance! Be sure to let your dance partner know that you are leaving the ballroom.

Get enough sleep the night before you compete or perform. This is easier said than done at big competitions, where you might have to dance at midnight and then get up the next day and dance again. But get as much sleep as you can—don't stay up late to party if you have to dance early the next day. You'll be glad you opted for sleep when you are rested and refreshed, rather than dragging with exhaustion. If you have trouble sleeping the night before you dance, due to excitement or jitters, lie down and rest in the dark even if you can't sleep. And focus your thoughts on something positive and pleasant, rather than worrying about how you placed today or might place tomorrow. Your body will thank you.

Grooming

When you are new to ballroom performance, grooming can be one of the hardest aspects to get used to. We all have certain styles of presenting ourselves that naturally reflect the way we wish to be seen. Many people who are used to presenting themselves rather conservatively in their business and professional life balk at the requirements of ballroom grooming when they are first introduced to them. And, let's face it, grooming is a much bigger challenge for the ladies than for the gentlemen. Overdone makeup, fake tanning, and thousands of rhinestones do not fit the image that most women have in mind when they are planning to be seen in public.

On the other hand, the "Cinderella" aspect of competing and performing is really part of the fun. We get to be little kids again, dressing up for Halloween, living a fairy tale, or pretending to attend a royal ball. Taken in this spirit, the women really can have more fun with grooming than the men, because the gentleman's grooming is so boring by comparison. The men dress in black to frame the lady, while the women get to wear fabulous designer gowns.

But women may have to work harder to overcome their inhibitions about appearing "inappropriate" than the men do. Skimpy Latin costumes, for example, may make some women feel quite uncomfortable. (More about choosing a costume below.)

Overdone makeup may carry negative associations about being mistaken for *that* sort of woman... But if you think of a ballroom dance performance as theater, it may be easier to make the mental shift required to go full out with grooming.

As on the stage, what looks overdone close up looks great from further away, just as brush strokes on a canvas can look garish at close range but become a beautiful painting when viewed from the proper distance. The bright lights *will* wash out your coloring if you are not tanned and overly made up. If you are a naturally dark-complexioned person, you are lucky—you get to skip the tanning. But for fair-skinned people, it is important to tan with self-tanning products or makeup in order to achieve the proper "ballroom look."

It is very helpful to attend a competition as a spectator, in order to see that the grooming that is acceptable for "normal life" looks out of place on the competition floor. Pay attention to what looks good from a distance. What colors stand out? Which costumes enhance the dancing, and which distract from it? What kinds of ballroom shoes are being worn?

We once knew a student who wanted to compete, but refused to tan. The teacher would not allow her to participate if she wasn't willing to tan, and she left the studio. That may sound harsh, but from the teacher's point of view, the un-tanned student would have reflected poorly on her guidance. Unfair as this seems, it is true. If you attend a competition and see students who are not tanned, made up, coiffed, and costumed according to prevailing ballroom standards, people will say, "Poor thing, she's not getting the right advice! Why didn't her teacher give her more help with grooming?"

Your grooming is your responsibility. This means finding out what is expected and learning to do it. This goes for both members of the partnership. If you are new to ballroom grooming, you should practice grooming, just as you would practice dancing. Try different products to see which ones you like. Ask more experienced dancers whose look you admire what they use. You don't want to have an allergic reaction to your hairspray at the competition! (And do use fake tanning products—real tanning with ultra violet rays can damage and age your skin.)

If you are lucky enough to be attending a competition where professional hair and makeup services are offered, you may want to schedule an appointment. Be aware that the people offering these services can get very busy and backed up, so you not only need to schedule in advance, you should take a slot that is well ahead of when you need to be in the ballroom. (Betty had a hair appointment at 5:00 AM in her bronze days—a great incentive to move up to a higher level so she could sleep later and dance later in the day!) Over time, you will probably want to learn to do this for yourself, not only to save money, but because if you are at a smaller or all-amateur competition, these services may not be available.

You will need attire appropriate to the style(s) you are dancing. Listen to your professionals about your choices. If you are a newcomer, you will benefit from their experience. If you see a gown that appeals to you, show it to your teacher before you buy it.

It is acceptable ballroom etiquette to ask a lady wearing a gown you admire whether it is for sale. Many dancers buy pre-owned gowns; it is more economical than buying a new dress.

What works in your normal life may fade into the woodwork on the dance floor. If the judges don't see you, they can't mark you. Light or bright colors are best for the ladies. Dark colors tend to blend into the gentleman's black outfit. Ballroom outfits are gaudy and overdone by everyday standards, but they can still be flattering and in good taste. Choose something that looks good on you. If you don't feel comfortable in a revealing gown, choose one that covers more of you. You won't look good if you feel embarrassed about what you are wearing.

Take an honest look at yourself in the mirror. Emphasize your assets and cover your flaws. If you don't have good legs, for example, avoid really short Latin outfits. And make sure your costume fits. Tugging and pulling at costumes riding up or sliding off distracts you and the audience from your dancing.

Once you have chosen what you will wear, practice in it. The feeling of wearing a tail suit or a ball gown is quite different from the feeling of dancing in a t-shirt or a leotard. Both partners need practice to get used to the feeling of a new outfit. Some women's costumes have moving parts—sleeves that can fly into the man's face during an underarm turn, or dangles from the waist or skirt that can whip into his legs—or even into her own. If you need to make adjustments for flying costume parts you will want to find this out in advance, not discover it during a performance! Even the process of getting dressed should be practiced. It may take you longer than you expected to put all those studs into a shirt and collar, and some women's costumes have complicated systems of straps, hooks, and snaps that require help. Leave plenty of time for getting dressed and made up— much more than you think you need. At a competition your heat can be called as early as 30 minutes before the scheduled time. That means you need to be in the ballroom, ready to dance, a minimum of 45 minutes before your heat is scheduled. If you glue your eyelashes on crooked, you don't want to be in a panic about taking the time to remove them and start over.

Grooming Errors

"But," we can hear you asking, "shouldn't they be judging the dancing, not the grooming?" Yes, at a competition, the judges do judge the dancing. But consider that dancing is a visual art. Your appearance is part of the picture. If someone who is poorly groomed is clearly dancing better than someone who is well-groomed, the better dancer will be marked higher. But if the level of dancing is close, then grooming can be the deciding factor in the placements.

We once attended a seminar by World Latin Champion Shirley Ballas. She was very clear that good grooming can make the difference in the judges' decision when couples are closely-matched in the dancing. She said she will even look at whether the lady's finger and toe nail polish matches, and whether the polish is chipped!

Grooming can even make a difference before you walk on to the dance floor. Couples with appropriate grooming (and good posture) make a better appearance just walking out from the "on deck" area than couples with poor grooming. Good ballroom grooming sends the message, "We belong here. We know what we are doing." Yes, you still have to back it up with good dancing, but good grooming makes a favorable first impression.

Conversely, grooming errors can distract from good dancing. You don't have to have an expensive costume, but you should present a neat and tidy appearance. We once attended a college competition where the grooming errors were numerous and obvious. Here are some of the things we saw that should never be seen at a performance or on a competitive dance floor unless they are part of an intentionally humorous showcase routine: shirt-tails untucked, hair messy and uncombed, safety pins showing, undergarments showing, ladies underarm hair and unshaved legs, unplanned gaps between tops and skirts, open snaps and zippers, gum chewing, and white socks with black shoes! One judge decided to just "go with the flow" of the informal atmosphere by wearing "bunny slippers" while judging! You would never see that at a regular competition.

Packing

Since grooming is so important, it follows that you must take responsibility for packing and transporting all the things you will need from your home to wherever you are dancing. This includes shoes, costumes, jewelry, makeup, hair products, a shoe brush, a warm-up jacket or robe to cover your costume while you are waiting, and anything else you need for your dancing. It is a really good idea to develop a system to help you remember everything you need. We keep a dance packing list on our computer, and update it as needed. Other dancers keep a pre-packed suitcase. Whatever system you use should work for you, so that you do not have to start from scratch every time you go somewhere to perform.

The vendors at a ballroom competition will be happy to sell you all the things you forgot to pack; the bigger the competition, the more vendors and the more choices. But what if you will be performing at a local venue with no vendors, or a small competition with few choices? And even at a big competition you don't want to have to shop under pressure at the last minute. It is much better to shop later, after you dance.

Because luggage can be delayed or even lost forever when you travel by air, we advise you never to check your dance costumes. Dresses can be rolled up small and carried in your hand luggage. Amazing as it may seem, they will shake out just fine and not be wrinkled. More experienced dancers will be happy to share their packing tips. The man's suit can fit into a carry-on garment bag. You really do not want to be in the situation of having to buy clothing that represents such a big investment at the competition, or of having to dance in your practice outfit.

We once saw a champion dancer, whose luggage had been delayed, compete in a practice outfit which didn't fit her well. She was still the best dancer, and she and her partner won, but there was negative gossip afterward about how she should not have competed without proper costuming. The judges felt it was disrespectful toward the event.

Be Prepared for Dance Disasters

Speaking of lost luggage, if you attend enough dance competitions, you will have lots of chances to see "dance disasters." Earrings fly off, nails and zippers break, shoes disintegrate, hair comes undone, costumes rip or get caught in the partner's costume—we've seen almost everything. Some of them shouldn't appear in print. And the things we haven't seen, we've heard about (ask us...).

> The human story does not always unfold like a mathematical calculation on the principle that two and two make four. Sometimes in life they make five or minus three; and sometimes the blackboard topples down in the middle of the sum and leaves the class in disorder and the pedagogue with a black eye.
>
> *Winston Churchill*

So it would be wise to plan for anything that could possibly go wrong, and have a backup plan. One time, Betty put her heel through her dress while doing a quick run-through with Art at the side of the ballroom a half-hour before we were to dance. Luckily, she had her sewing kit (containing thread to match each costume) in her dance bag. She was able to do a credible repair on the spot in the ballroom without taking off the dress.

Another time we were all set to dance our solo number when the music failed to work. Since solos are choreographed to specific music, when you are dancing a solo routine at a competition you provide your own music. So there we were, all set up on the huge dance floor at Cobo Hall, ready to perform, when the person running the music said, "I'm sorry, but your tape just broke." "Don't worry, we said, we have another copy." The backup copy was with us in the ballroom. It took only a moment to get it, and on we went, to major applause.

Dance disasters can cause stressful moments, but they make the best stories later. Be as prepared as possible for anything to go wrong. If it does, handle it as best you can, and support each other through it without blaming each other. Later, you can have a good laugh.

Responsiveness

Competition and performance put partnership to the test. Everyone gets some jitters before a performance; this is normal, natural, and, in moderation, even helpful. We have prepared for this moment, and we want to look good and do our best. Our adrenaline is flowing. Our focus turns inward as we prepare, doing our grooming, stretching, double-checking that we have all our supplies (including backups), and mentally reviewing our choreography and technique. As we become self-absorbed in the stress of the moment, it is easy to be impatient with our partner—but this is when we need each other most of all.

Because of our focus on ourselves when we are nervous before performing, it can be difficult to tune in to each other. So being explicit in our communication can be especially helpful at this point. Ask and tell. This is no time to mind-read. "How are you doing?" "Do you need anything from me?" "I'm going over to that corner to stretch." "I'm going to the restroom." "I'm going to get water, would you like some?" "We have ten heats before we go on; it's time to move near the on-deck area." "I'd like to set up with you in dance position just to get the feeling of being together."

You get the idea. Be explicit. Be clear. Be complimentary. "You look wonderful!" "I'm looking forward to dancing with you!"

Controlling Performance Jitters

If performance jitters get out of hand, they can interfere with your partnership, your dancing, and your fun. Getting a handle on these involves taking individual responsibility for learning how to master your anxiety, as well as receiving a supportive response from a patient and understanding partner. If you begin to snap and snipe at each other, the partnership loses.

Mastering performance jitters is not easy. It requires repeated practice using a two-pronged approach. First is the mental or philosophical part, and second is the concrete behavioral aspect.

Anxiety is critical for survival. Think about it—we are descended from the people who *weren't* eaten by the saber-toothed tiger. We descended from the people who looked out for danger. But modern life in a developed country (one with ballroom dancing!) is generally safe, so most of us have more anxiety than we really need for our day-to-day safety. This excess anxiety can float around and become focused on things that have no life-or-death consequences—like our dancing.

This echoes back to the issue of perfectionism, which we discussed in Chapter 1. We will never be perfect. We will never perform flawlessly. This is a fact we must accept. The "upside" is that everyone is in the same boat. The judges understand this. They don't expect perfection; rather, they give favorable marks to couples who can recover well from an error.

> Striving for excellence motivates you; striving for perfection is demoralizing.
>
> *Harriet Braiker*

Remember—the object of all the lessons, practice, and hours of training is to enjoy yourself on the dance floor. Competing and performing are just ways to share that enjoyment with others. Let yourself enjoy the feeling of dancing. Allow it to crowd out any other feeling. When you make the inevitable mistake, try not to show that it's not what you had planned. It is fun to watch people who are enjoying themselves, even if they aren't perfect. So *be* that person who is fun to watch because they are having fun. Allow your enjoyment to show. Dance the board you are on, that is, let any previous error go, and move on. There is always the next round.

OK, once you have readied your attitude it is time to put into concrete practice behaviors that mirror your positive philosophical outlook. *Enact* through behavior the attitudes you are trying to cultivate. Historically, there has been a chicken-and-egg controversy in psychology over whether changing your behavior can change your feelings and thoughts, or whether you have to change your feelings and cognitions (thoughts and ideas) before you can change your behavior. It turns out that it can work in either direction. For example, you don't have to wait until you stop feeling anxious to smile. If you smile and act confident, it will actually help you feel less anxious.

> Sometimes your joy is the source of your smile, but sometimes your smile can be the source of your joy.
>
> *Thich Nhat Hanh*

So when you are getting ready to perform, smile, and focus on your partner. Walk onto the floor as if you own it—proud, happy, and visibly confident. Gentlemen, indicate your skill with firm but gentle control as you place your lady on the floor. Clear placement gives the lady confidence in you and helps her to relax and focus. As the music begins, pick up your posture, puff out your chest, and convey a positive intention as you welcome your lady into your arms. Invite her to dance with you in a way that says you mean it. You are dancing with the prettiest woman in the ballroom! Welcome her with a smile worthy of that awareness. Smile in anticipation of having a wonderful experience. And, just maybe, you will.

Ladies, smile with pleasure in response. Think of all those women who tell you how jealous they are that you get to dance! You have practiced, you are prepared, you look beautiful. Your partner is the handsomest man in the ballroom. Now have a wonderful time!

In addition to smiling, the other behavior you need to practice is breathing. This may sound silly—we breathe all the time without thinking about it. But we all have a tendency to hold our breath when we are concentrating really hard. This is actually counterproductive, reducing the flow of oxygen to the brain and the muscles. What we need to train ourselves to do, instead, is to breathe deeply and with awareness. Deep, slow breaths actually induce a physiologic response called "the relaxation response."

> The only difference between fear and excitement is whether you're breathing.
>
> *Dan Millman*

Remember the exercise in Chapter 2, "Practicing Posture and Self Respect"? This exercise is one way to produce the relaxation response. If you practice it on a regular basis, you will find it easier to get to a relaxed and centered place when you perform or compete. Just slowly blowing out the breath can be a short-cut way to "remind" your body of that relaxed feeling. Your heart rate will drop and you will feel more calm and in control. Watch close-ups of the faces of Olympic athletes such as skiers and skaters just before they compete. It is quite common to see them take a moment to exhale fully before they begin.

So breathe—smile—enjoy. You'll have a wonderful time. And the more times you perform and compete, the more familiar and less frightening it will seem.

Attunement during the Performance

So what happens if you are actually out there in front of people and something goes wrong? Don't worry, the more you perform and compete, the more experiences you *will* have of things going wrong—and the more opportunities you will have to "cover" for each other and not let the mistakes show. This is where responsiveness in the partnership really pays off. If you and your partner are truly "tuned in" to each other, you will automatically work together in the moment. We have so many stories ...

For example, there was the time another couple cut between us in an American style foxtrot routine where we were dancing apart. Betty got to the end of the long side and turned, but Art wasn't there to take her hand! She saw that he had been delayed, and vamped until he got there. Art, meanwhile, improvised a running step to get where he needed to be, and we picked up the routine when he got there. The whole thing probably only took an extra measure, but it was a fun and exciting challenge to make it work, and we got lots of cheers from the audience!

Another time, when Betty was dancing pro-am with Louis, he coached her between rounds to be more aggressive in the tango in the next round. Without planning it, all of a sudden Betty began improvising something aggressive in the middle of her tango! Louis followed flawlessly, then they got back into the routine. Who says men can't follow! (And with relatively good humor.)

In a good partnership, couples don't get hung up on who is leading in the middle of a performance. As we said in Chapter 4, the more experienced you become, the more you pass the "lead" back and forth between you; dancing together flows from leading and following into tuning in and matching. Performing gives us an opportunity to take responsibility for our own dancing no matter what happens. We focus on making the partnership work and making it look easy. We smile as we handle whatever challenges appear in the moment. In fact, once we accept the reality that errors can and will happen at any time, we can greet them as fun opportunities, put on the show, and dance with joy!

> Joy is what happens when we allow ourselves to recognize how good things are. Joy is not necessarily what happens when things unfold according to our plans.
>
> *Marianne Williamson*

Review of Applying Relationship Skills in Performance and Competition

Respect

* Respect yourself
* Respect your partner
* Respect the organizers and judges
* Respect other dancers
* Respect the activity

Responsibility

* Practice
* Physical preparation
* Grooming
* Grooming errors
* Packing
* Be prepared for dance disasters

Responsiveness

* Controlling performance jitters
* Attunement during the performance

Gold Level Relationship Fitness—
Advanced Practice

Chapter 11

GOLD LEVEL RESPECT: RADICALLY RESPECTING REALITY

The gold level of relationship fitness is not for everyone. You can lead a perfectly happy, normal life, without digging deeply into the relationship issues that we will take up at the gold/advanced level. So if you want to stop here, you can still get a great deal of use from this book just by reading the first ten chapters and practicing respect, responsibility, and responsiveness at the bronze and silver levels. Just as with dance levels, you can have a wonderful time while remaining in bronze or silver.

> I believe in looking reality straight in the eye and denying it.
>
> *Garrison Keillor*

At the bronze and silver levels we can practice respectful behavior without needing to believe, deep down, that our dance problems are not our partner's fault. And in most relationships, just behaving in a more respectful way and keeping some of our (negative) true feelings to ourselves is good enough. In fact, for many people it is a huge improvement over their usual behavior. Art found in his therapeutic work with couples, for example, that just helping them to say "please" and "thank you" to each other had a profound positive effect on their relationship, though it often took a long time and a lot of discussion for them to try it.

If a couple wants to achieve a deeper level of partnership, however, they may wish to move to the level of *radically respecting reality*. Radically respecting reality means accepting the world as it is. It means viewing our relationships, and our world, without defensiveness. Simple, no? No.

> The first step toward change is awareness. The second step is acceptance.
>
> *Nathaniel Branden*

Acceptance vs. Resignation

So what do we mean by accepting reality? Must acceptance mean resignation to things as they are? Certainly not! We mean having a non-defensive attitude toward whatever is happening, both internally and externally. This involves learning to take responsibility for our own behavior, rather than defending ourselves or attacking our partner. When we respect reality, we move beyond the need to attack or defend. Instead, we pay attention to what is happening within ourselves and our relationships.

In Chapter 1 we noted that dancing is an activity that assaults our psychological defenses, which typically operate automatically, outside of our awareness. We can think of them as operating through stories, beliefs, and judgments we carry around internally:

"He looked at me and smiled. He likes me."

"She looked at me and looked away. What a bitch!"

"That food is unfamiliar. It's gross."

"I've always been clumsy. I'd never learn to be a dancer."

"She's always late. She is so irresponsible." And so on.

As we move through life we are constantly assessing and categorizing our experiences. There is great efficiency in these cognitive habits. We can imagine that they were very important for our cave ancestors:

"Here is a plant; is it edible, inedible, or poisonous? Not sure. Better not eat it."

"There is a noise. Is it a predator? I must be prepared to fight or flee!"

But distortion is the downside to this efficiency. Our brain is designed to simplify information in order to make it more manageable. We all have a strong preference for fitting new experiences—whether perceptions, thoughts, or feelings—into categories we have already developed. This is the basis of prejudice: "They are all lazy." "All they think about is money," and so on. It takes less effort to squeeze the square peg of experience into the round hole of our existing ideas than it does to constantly build new holes to fit. But when we distort our experiences in order to fit them into our existing ideas, we stray from reality. We feel temporarily comfortable, because it can give us the illusion that we are always "right," but it can also be dangerous. Whenever we say "no" to reality, we are fighting what is.

> When I argue with reality, I lose—but only 100 percent of the time.
> **Byron Katie**

So what does accepting reality look like? It involves noting our experience and then pausing to let it flow through us without judging, categorizing, or telling ourselves a story about it. Let's say, for example, I notice I am tired. A judging reaction might be to say, internally, "You fool! How could you stay up so late last night! You know better than that!" Categorizing might involve telling myself, "You are getting older. You just don't have the same energy you used to." If I told myself a story about being tired, I might begin to make it into a catastrophe, saying something like, "Oh, dear. Now I won't have enough energy to dance well and I'll disappoint my partner, myself, my teacher, and all my relatives." Accepting my tiredness would involve simply noting it, without having to make it into anything else. This would actually be less tiring than any of the other alternatives.

Accepting reality involves letting go of our old stories and opening ourselves to new experiences. For example, we could change, "I've always been clumsy. I'll never learn to be a good dancer," to, "Perhaps I can learn to move so that I will feel more graceful." Or, "Do I really care whether others think I'm graceful? I want to dance."

Art remembers hearing an inspiring interview with an Australian figure skater in the Winter Olympics some years back after she came in last in her event. Was she depressed by her placement? On the contrary, "I knew I would probably come in last," she said. "I had no coach, no costume designer, no choreographer, and hardly any place to practice. But I was thrilled just to be able to compete in the Olympics!" She showed that she not only respected and accepted reality, she embraced and celebrated it! And she had a wonderful experience she'd remember the rest of her life.

Accepting reality involves refraining from making judgments about other people's motives and, instead, checking out their version of reality, or, at least, recognizing the difference between what has occurred and the story we are telling ourselves about what has occurred. Using the example above, instead of thinking, "She looked at me and looked away. What a bitch!" I might seek information. "How are you? Are you doing OK?" Then I might find out that she feels ill, is preoccupied with other thoughts, didn't see me, or is, indeed, not interested in interacting with me right then. With more accurate information I could then make a more informed decision about what to do next. Recognizing and accepting "what is" opens up the possibility of choice and change. Accepting reality is empowering.

> We cannot change anything until we accept it. Condemnation does not liberate, it oppresses.
>
> *C. G. Jung*

Reality and Perfectionism

In Chapter 1 we talked about how dancing tends to activate the psychological issues we all have in the areas of perfectionism and blame. Unlike adding a column of numbers and coming up with the correct sum, in dancing, as in life, a "perfect" outcome is impossible. Does this mean we must always be dissatisfied? How could respecting reality be applied to perfectionism?

> Imperfection is not our personal problem— it is a natural part of existing.
>
> *Tara Brach*

Slow down, breathe, and think: if the reality is that perfect dancing is impossible, we are left with two choices—either we can distort reality and believe that our dancing is, or can be, perfect; or we can accept that our dancing is, and always will be, imperfect. And what then? If we accept imperfection as reality, this can free us to set more realistic goals. Instead of trying to be "perfect" and blaming someone (ourselves, our partner, our coach) when we fall short, we can focus our energy and attention on some small area we are trying to improve. Maybe it is a low-energy day for us. We might decide that our goal for that dance experience is just to keep our frame toned as well as we can. Or maybe our focus is just to have a good time and enjoy the dancing.

Or we could redefine perfection as happiness. (Oh, were there more than two choices? Yes, always...) We could choose to notice that life is often beautiful, that when the birds are singing and the sun is shining, and we are healthy enough to walk the earth and breathe the air, life is perfect enough.

> Happiness is when what you think, what you say, and what you do are in harmony.
>
> *Mahatma Gandhi*

Another, even more radical possibility, would be to let go of the idea that there can ever be such a thing as perfection. What if we gave up the fairy tale and recognized that "perfection" is just a mental construct? Maybe "perfection," like Cinderella and Goldilocks, is just another story we tell ourselves to keep us from embracing reality. And maybe we don't need this fairy tale. Maybe we can just love life with all its imperfections.

> I have found that if you love life, life will love you back.
>
> *Arthur Rubenstein*

Or, another radical idea: maybe perfection is boring. We once had coaching from John Nyemchek. We were bronze dancers, just starting out, and most of what he tried to convey was way over our heads, but we remember to this day one idea he emphasized: "You see those speakers over there on the floor? They are in perfect balance. All this furniture is in perfect balance. We know this because it doesn't fall over. But it's not interesting to watch. Perfection is boring. Show me something interesting to watch."

Wow! What a concept! Perfection is not just impossible, it's also boring! This is why people still buy tickets to hear live music performances when they could buy a CD for less money, listen to it in the comfort of their own home, and hear a perfect rendition. Digital recordings are perfected by having individual notes taken out and corrected, so that the normal flaws of a live performance are gone. But the natural imperfections of reality are more exciting, engaging, and enjoyable to see and hear.

> You see, when weaving a blanket, an Indian woman leaves a flaw in the weaving of that blanket to let the soul out.
>
> *Martha Graham*

Reality and Blame

Blame is the "other half" of perfectionism (see Chapter 1). If we can truly let go of our perfectionism, blame will become a foreign idea. Neither of us is to blame, because the concept of blame is irrelevant. Each of us is who and what we are at any given moment. Each of us is doing the best we can at that moment, or we'd be doing something else. Respect that.

> Mistakes fail in their mission of helping the person who blames them on the other fellow.
>
> *Henry S. Haskins*

No one gets up in the morning saying, "My plan is to dance badly today so that I can annoy my dance partner." If you truly feel this about your partner, you are with the wrong person (and so is your partner...). If you don't feel this way, then give your partner the benefit of the doubt when things aren't going well. Go beyond respect—treat him or her with kindness and compassion. The tables will be turned on you soon enough.

"But," we can hear you protesting, "how can we ever improve? If I just accept myself and my partner as we are, doesn't that mean complacency and the end of growth?"

On the contrary. Embracing reality and letting go of blame allows us to let go of the stories that distract us from focusing on whatever we are choosing to work on. We all waste so much time and energy on those old, tired stories we have always told ourselves. We become fond of them; they feel as comfortable as worn slippers. But we don't need them any more.

Art says: I have told at least three different therapists all about how my parents never taught me the foreign languages they spoke. Boo hoo! Only later in life did it occur to me—what are you waiting for? You can take charge. If you really want to learn a language, buy and book and a dictionary and teach yourself! Which is just what I did.

> Perfection, fortunately, is not the only alternative to mediocrity. A more sensible alternative is excellence. Striving for excellence is stimulating and rewarding; striving for perfection—in practically anything—is both neurotic and futile.
>
> *Edwin Bliss*

When we lift the veil of blame and begin to look clearly, we stop projecting our internal issues onto our partner, who then becomes a real person to us. This frees us to become more curious about and interested in our partner. As we release our attachment to our own point of view, a kinder, more compassionate attention will flow naturally.

Does that sound weird? Most of the time it is very hard to see people as they really are, separate from ourselves and our stories. Our habit is to constantly assess everyone in relation to ourselves.

Accepting that our partner is truly someone else, who is experiencing life differently, can be tremendously liberating. We can begin to see that our different approaches to problems are not just because the other person is so wrong, or even that we have different points of view, *we are actually experiencing different versions of reality*. Does this sound familiar? Remember staying on your own side and minding your own business from Chapter 3? This is the next step. Not only is my partner having a different experience, but that experience, in combination with my partner's personal history, is actually creating a different personal version of reality. How exciting! Two versions of reality where we imagined there was only one before!

How can that be? Here's a simple example. She says, "The ballroom is too cold." He says, "No, the ballroom is too hot!" The reality is that the ballroom temperature is 70 degrees Fahrenheit. So who is "right?" They are both "right" about their own experience, but each of them has misspoken. The ballroom temperature is 70 degrees. It is neither too hot nor too cold; those are judgments each person is making.

We habitually speak from our own point of view as if that point of view represents reality. This habit encourages us to believe that our point of view *is* a representation of reality. Once we realize that our point of view is only our own reality, we can begin to train ourselves to speak more accurately (for example, "I feel cold" instead of, "The ballroom is too cold"). We can, as well, learn to translate, internally, what others say. For example, "When he says, 'The ballroom is too hot,' he means, 'I feel too hot.'"

When she says, "Don't push me!" it probably means he is dropping his frame.

With this system, no one is "right" and no one is "wrong"; we are just having different experiences. What a saving of psychic energy. We don't always have to be right. We can save ourselves the pain of those "dance spats." But to find out about our partner's version of reality, we really need those "I-Messages."

Seeking Reality with "I-Messages"

Listen to the way people speak about any topic. (Yes, all of us.) Judgments are constantly being made, stories told, and complexities oversimplified. We do it because it makes us feel like we know things. It gives us the illusion of control. We do it to entertain ourselves and each other, and we do it to comfort ourselves. We do it to form and maintain social relationships, including our place in our social hierarchy. It is fun, interesting, and engaging. All of this is fine as long as we also know, at another level, that very little of this discourse is a representation of reality.

> Don't believe everything you think.
>
> *Thomas Kida*

We all have to be careful about believing our own stories. The more we repeat them, the more we believe them, and the more they tend to crowd out our real experiences. Our verbal habits are so strong that it can be very hard for us to allow ourselves to experience our sensory and body feelings directly. One of the great values of dancing is that it is a direct body experience that takes us away from our world of words. Among the many gifts that dancing gives us is an immediate, exquisite attunement with another person without using words. Words can actually be a barrier to experience (remember "The Words Get in the Way" from Chapter 8?).

On the other hand, in order to learn, we need to rely on verbal communication, with all its inadequacy. Learning is often frustrating. As we try to improve, we are likely to become irritated with ourselves, our partner, or our teacher, and to respond by judging and blaming, either internally or externally.

In Chapter 6 we described how to use "I-Messages" during a dance spat. If you have tried this, you may have found that, like any dance skill, it becomes easier and feels more natural with time and practice. It is likely that you have experienced the pleasant surprise of achieving a better outcome when you exercised respectful self control. An "I-Message" has worked in a situation that, in the past, had typically spiraled downward.

At the bronze and silver levels of relationship fitness, simply using "I-Messages" is enough. At a gold/advanced level, however, we can take this one step further. Although we know that we can never experience our partner's reality, nor they ours, we can extend ourselves with true open-mindedness, moving beyond *tolerating* to truly *valuing* our separate realities: "Here is my experience. What is your experience?" "I feel this, what do you feel?"

This can be a fascinating exercise, which need not be reserved for problem situations, but can be used whenever we become aware of the possibility of seeing the world from a different point of view.

All of us experience life in our own, unique way, filtered through the lens of our previous experience and present perception. Partnered dancing is particularly likely to uncover and expose the existence of our separate realities because the lady and the gentleman have different roles and responsibilities within the dance. Even though we are working together, it is obvious that we are doing different things. At best, we fit together and complement each other beautifully. We are the *yin* and the *yang*. The physical movements of the dance enable us to enact separate realities overtly. And then we can ask each other what that is like.

Betty, for example, finds it difficult to do anything that feels "rude." If she felt that what she was being asked to do in the dance would physically "impose" on Art, she used to hang back, rather than dancing fully. Now she has learned to ask him, if she is dancing in a way that feels too aggressive to her, "I'm wondering what that is like for you. Does it bother you?" Quite often Art will say that he didn't even notice it because he was too busy focusing on what he was trying to do, himself. At other times he says he likes it—that it feels better or "lighter." This, of course, is the purpose of better technique—to make it easier for the couple. Because Betty checked out her "story" ("I'm being rude!") with Art, we are both able to enjoy the dancing more.

"Shoulds" Oppose Reality

"Should" is a wonderful word to watch out for. Whenever we say "should," whether externally or internally, we are fighting reality. This can be a truly useful warning signal.

How do "shoulds" fight reality? The whole concept of "should" is a challenge to what "is." For example, "Those children should be quiet." Really? If they "should" be, they would be. What we really mean is, "I wish those children would be quiet." Now we are representing the idea of quiet children as our wish, and taking responsibility for our wish. This more realistic way of thinking frees us to make a plan for action. Taking responsibility for our wish opens up possible new solutions. For example, move to a different spot, use ear plugs, approach the children in a friendly manner and engage them in conversation, or decide to enjoy the noise of children—whatever might be appropriate in the situation. Being bogged down in what someone else "should" be doing is blaming and disempowering (I don't need to take action because it is the other person who "should" change).

> God grant me the serenity to accept the things I cannot change, the courage to change the things I can, and the wisdom to know the difference.
>
> *Serenity Prayer*

"Shoulds" are code words for blame. Every "should" implies that someone is at fault. Blaming invites defense, whether we blame ourselves or others. Defense leads to hunkering down and reinforcing our positions—the opposite of change. Releasing our "shoulds" and transforming them into accurate statements radically respects reality and clarifies where and how change might be possible. For example, "I *should* do my footwork correctly," is accurate in one sense, but in another sense it is not. "I *should* do correct footwork," is a statement that carries no opening toward change—instead, it invites self-blame, which actually becomes a *substitute* for action.

"I *want* to improve my footwork"—Now, that is different. It leads to a plan of action. "*My coach* wants me to improve my footwork" invites a question. "Ah, but do *I* want to improve my footwork? If not, why not?" Such questions invite further exploration and understanding; then your decision is based on reality.

If we are courageous enough to be honest, surprising, wonderful things happen. Art, for example, felt at one stage that he didn't want to improve! When he discussed this frankly with Betty and their teacher, he was able to find a new way of understanding what was happening for him, and to change. Feeling like he didn't have to hide the "bad" feelings he was carrying was a tremendous relief. It gave him a surge of energy for dancing.

Other code words to watch out for are "always" and "never." There is an old humorous adage, "Always remember to never say always or never." But the message is serious—absolutes cannot be true. When they are applied to human behavior they "always" invite argument. Whenever you are tempted to say "I always," or "You never," watch out! Pause, breathe, and think of a more accurate and less extreme way to make your point.

Making Friends with Reality

In ballroom dancing we commonly say, "The floor is your friend." We would like to add a new adage: "Reality is your friend."

Fantasy can be fun. Wishes can be fun. But spending one's time and mental energy wishing and dreaming carries a hidden danger. When you are dreaming and wishing you are not "in" your own life; you are in a kind of trance. If you spend too much time there you miss your actual life. If you are a political prisoner or in a concentration camp, then that may be just what you want to do. But if you are reading this book, your reality is not as terrible as that.

In any case, you want to be in charge of the shift between fantasy and reality, rather than allowing the habit of daydreaming to be in charge of you; you then have the opportunity to use it constructively, which can lead to action.

Here is a simple example. We used to play a game: "What would we do if we won the lottery?" (Though of course, we never bought a ticket. We were just having fun spinning a shared fantasy to pass the time while traveling in the car.) We discovered two things: first, we were already pretty content with our lives, since it was hard to come up with new things we really wanted; and second, the things we really wanted were things we could decide to do, perhaps in a modified form, without having to win the lottery.

Betty, for example, thought that if she won the lottery she would like to have fresh flowers on her desk at work during the winter months. Then she thought, "I wonder how expensive that would be?" She looked into it and was surprised to find that she could afford it, so she began to buy flowers for her desk each week during the winter. Making that reality happen was far more satisfying than the fantasy of having flowers. Making friends with reality led to a satisfying action that increased her enjoyment in life.

This can be done with anything you think you wish for. Ask yourself, "Do I really wish that? What would it be like? What do I like about that idea?" Often, the more you subject your fantasy to scrutiny, the less attractive it seems. If you still really like it, find out more about what it would take to make it a reality. If you still like it, you could decide to make it happen based on good information.

Years ago we spun a shared fantasy of opening a restaurant we would call, "The Seagull's Nest." It would be nonsmoking (something that did not exist at the time). It would be located out in the country where we would grow our own organic vegetables and herbs for the set seasonal menu (also new ideas at the time). This idea seemed so delightful that Art called up a friend who owned a restaurant and asked him how much capital it would take to start such a restaurant. After a frank conversation about the realities of owning and running a restaurant, we decided it was definitely not for us. Yes, our fantasy bubble was popped by the tiny pin of reality—but how much better than if we had spent years seriously longing for this dream without doing anything to pursue it. We realized that what we really wanted was to be patrons at such a restaurant, not owners!

> Who is rich? One who is happy with his portion.
>
> *Pirke Avot*

Another aspect of making friends with reality is to learn to distinguish reality from what you think is reality. Often the power of our thinking seems so compelling that we mistake it for what is real. Just because I believe something, no matter how fervently, that doesn't necessarily make it real.

How does this apply to dancing? If you daydream about becoming a champion, then find out what the path is to becoming a champion. Once you understand the realities involved, decide whether you still want to pursue that dream. If you do, stop dreaming and start working.

> If the power to do hard work is not talent, it is the best possible substitute for it. Ambition by itself never gets anywhere until it forms a partnership with work.
>
> *James Garfield*

And if you want to know what your partner is thinking or feeling, ask—don't project. Then listen with respect. Let the reply sink in, and accept it without judging or defending. Resist the temptation to second-guess about underlying motives and hidden agendas. If you are still puzzled, ask another question with respect, caring, and a genuine interest in your partner's perception of reality. Let go of having to be "right" or convincing your partner of anything. Be really there with him or her in the moment. You may be surprised to discover how good this feels.

Reality is all we have. This is our life, here and now. Embrace it with joy. Be realistic about what is within your power and let go of what is not. Make the changes you want in yourself. Then reality will truly be your friend.

> Paradise is where I am.
>
> *Voltaire*

Review of Gold Level Respect: Radically Respecting Reality

Accepting reality does not mean resignation
* Moving beyond defensiveness
* Letting go of judging, categorizing, and distorting

Letting go of perfectionism is freeing
* Perfection is impossible
* Perfection is boring

Blame is irrelevant
* We all experience our own reality
* We need to be careful about believing our own stories
* We need to use I-messages
* We can value our partner's different experience

"Shoulds" oppose reality

Reality is your friend

Chapter 12

GOLD LEVEL RESPONSIBILITY: ACCEPTING CRITICISM

> I love criticism just so long as it's unqualified praise.
>
> *Noel Coward*

We began the first chapter by observing that partnered dancing tends to assault psychological defenses. Criticism, by its very nature, attacks our carefully constructed sense of ourselves. Most of us walk around with a complex combination of contradictory ideas about ourselves, which includes both exaggerated views of how wonderful we are *and* exaggerated views of how awful we are. The truth, as we observed in Chapter 8, lies somewhere in-between.

Openness to Coaching

When we take up dancing, we expect to have fun, and we may be aware that it is good for our health, but most of us probably don't expect personal growth to be one of the outcomes. Yet dancing can teach us to accept and benefit from criticism. As with any art or sport, we can improve our performance by taking coaching from experts who look at what we are doing with a critical eye, analyze strengths and weaknesses, and suggest ways to make our dancing stronger. We obviously value it, after all, we pay a lot to receive this feedback; and yet—there's that six-year-old inside us. Where did that brat come from?!

Consider the problem that dance teachers and coaches face. To teach they must correct (criticize), yet they know how common it is for students to argue with them. Our "default" reaction to correction is defense: "What? I did take a heel lead." "I did syncopate that turn."

Or, we blame our partner: "I'm wonderful but my partner's dancing made it impossible for me to show you what a terrific dancer I am."

> Honest criticism is hard to take, particularly from a relative, a friend, an acquaintance, or a stranger.
>
> *Franklin P. Jones*

Either type of defense squanders time and money. When feelings are most intense, arguing with the coach can escalate into anger or tears. Yes, we want to be better dancers, but we don't want to change.

Wait—*what? You mean we want to change without changing? But that makes no sense!*

Ah, exactly. Now we are getting somewhere.

Resistance to Change

Why on earth would we resist change? There are so many reasons. Three that keep cropping up in our dancing are neophobia, fear of failure, and habit.

Neophobia

Neophobia is the fear of anything new. When we are suspicious of, or resistant to, new ideas or new ways of doing things—that's neophobia. All animals, including humans, show this to some extent. Have you ever put a new bird feeder in your backyard? It takes the birds a couple of days to get used to it before they trust it enough to approach it.

Neophobia is a big factor that stands in the way of change—and creativity. It keeps us in our safe little box where everything feels familiar and predictable.

You can see neophobia operating in its most simple and evident form in very young children, who are, by nature, quite vigilant about any departure from the familiar. They are, at best, suspicious of anything new. At the extreme, they are highly resistant. Here's a simple example: Betty was preparing some fresh strawberries for a snack for our two-year-old grandson. As she began cutting off the green tops, she heard a shriek, "No, Bubbe! That's not the way!"

Of course, we were amused and happy to accommodate to his idea that there was only one proper way to cut a strawberry—the way his parents do it. As adults we can understand how silly this is when we see a young child react this way. It is less easy and amusing to see it in ourselves.

You recall that in Chapter 11, we said there was survival value for our cave ancestors to develop habits that would enable them to quickly separate something unfamiliar into two large categories: the safe and the edible, versus the poisonous and dangerous. We said that the downside to this habit of thought is that it introduces distortion. What we didn't point out is that this habit is designed to err on the side of safety. If I eat a mushroom that is poisonous, I will die (severely cutting down on my chances of reproducing). If I pass up one that is edible, I may be a little hungry, but I may live long enough to be a parent. Therefore, suspicion toward the unfamiliar had survival value. We are descended from neophobes. It is bred deep within us.

Often we do not even know it is operating. Try this experiment: the next time someone tells you about a new idea, pay attention to your inner reaction. Do you feel excited about the new idea? Or is your first reaction to think of objections—why it doesn't make sense or wouldn't work? If you are like most people, the second type of reaction is your "default" mode. We tend to label people who embrace new ideas readily as naïve. A "wait and see" attitude is commonly regarded as more sensible and sophisticated. Most of us want to play it safe.

Fear of Failure

Fear of failure is another reason we resist change. As the saying goes, "If you do what you've always done, you'll get what you always got." But even if we are not satisfied with what we've always got, it is, at least, familiar, and we have learned to manage our feelings about it by using our psychological defenses. Making a radical departure from the familiar might result in a huge success—or a miserable failure. Most of us prefer to avoid the risk of a big failure.

Those who move outside of what is safe and known, the big risk-takers, expose themselves to hard falls as they seek big rewards. Stories of investing and inventing are full of tales of people who experienced many spectacular failures before they finally struck it rich with a big success.

Thomas Edison's mother removed him from school at age seven because his teacher had labeled him a slow learner. She didn't accept the judgment of the teacher, the authority. Perhaps it was from this example that her son learned to be an independent thinker. As an adult, Edison tried thousands of different materials before he finally found the right material for the filament in the first incandescent light bulb. He had learned to trust himself, rather than being daunted by the negative opinions of others. And he had learned to keep trying. The big risk-taker must be willing to turn a deaf ear to ridicule, whether internal or external. The big risk-taker needs both courage and persistence.

There are also many stories like this in the arts. Almost all artists who appear to others as "overnight successes" have actually spent years honing their craft before becoming successful. And those few who were child prodigies are often unable to sustain success because they relied too much on talent and never developed the habits of hard work, persistence—and audacity.

Habit

Humans are creatures of habit. Once we get into a rhythm of doing something in a certain way, we like doing it that way. There is a soothing quality about the repetition of a familiar habit. Art likes to grind the beans for our morning coffee for exactly 18 seconds every day. We figure out the most efficient route to drive from home to the office; then we go that way every day, annoyed if there is a detour for road repair. We find a store we like; then we prefer to shop there.

Habits represent cognitive efficiency. You don't have to think about brushing your teeth once you know how to do it. This frees up your brain for thinking. Our brains were designed for this—the more we do routine tasks by habit, the more we free up our intellect for other tasks—the original multitasking.

The more often a habit is repeated, the stronger and more automatic it becomes. The neurons fire and we do a task almost entirely outside of our awareness. This is both the benefit and the drawback of habit. As long as we want to keep the habit, the mindlessness of its execution is the hallmark of its efficiency. (How *do* we tie our shoelaces?) But when we want to change it—watch out. The habit which has worn a strong neural pathway in our brain is very hard to change. This is the essence of "muscle memory." We can see it when we do an ordinary task. How often have you meant to stop off and do an errand on your way home and forgotten because you were on "automatic pilot" as the car "drove itself" straight home?

This is the same thing that happens when you try to change a dance habit. If you have been doing something one way for a long time, the principles that apply to habit change are operating: (1) the habit occurs mostly outside of your awareness; (2) even though you have every intention of changing the habit, your body will resist and default to the familiar habit; (3) you must maintain heightened awareness and focused intention to develop a new habit; (4) the new behavior must be overpracticed before the old habit is replaced.

Changing well-established habits is a very frustrating process! Once we move beyond our initial defensiveness about how we really *are* doing the technique correctly, we may feel angry at ourselves for not being able to make the change right away. Once the coach has explained it and we accept and understand what our bodies are being asked to do, we often find that, although we can reproduce the new move initially, once we try to incorporate it as we dance, we return to our old habit. Our good intentions are not enough. As Charlie Brown says, "Aaaaargh!" And if you think *you* are frustrated, that goes double for your dance partner if the habit is one that affects his or her dancing.

Perfectionism

Oh, no, not that again! Are you getting sick of thinking about perfectionism? Yes, so are we. We started talking about perfectionism in Chapter 1 and we're still not done. We'll only truly be able to let go of our perfectionism when we are completely bored by it. (We won't be perfect by then, but we won't care anymore.)

Changing a habit is very, very, difficult. We cannot change ourselves without taking responsibility for our behavior. Taking responsibility for our behavior can feel like blame, and, to the perfectionist, can feel extremely painful—far more painful than the situation objectively warrants. We perfectionists have a tendency to create our own pain. We set up little internal "tests" (for example, "I have to play this scale flawlessly ten times in a row. If I don't do it, it means I'm a hopeless failure and I will give up music."). Setting up such an internal test falsely raises the stakes of what is at risk. Reality is replaced by the fantasied test of worthiness. This, in turn, overloads the situation with anxiety, virtually guaranteeing failure—which becomes a self-fulfilling prophecy.

Dancing is a vehicle that can help us with these issues. People who voluntarily take on new challenges (like learning to dance) tend to be people who like to challenge themselves. This is even more true of those who go in for competitive dancing, since this is an optional activity.

Any hobby or sport presents opportunities to work on our perfectionism issues constructively. The truth is that we like to be good at things. We enjoy the feeling of mastery that comes with learning, especially learning something difficult.

If we can develop an attitude of compassion and acceptance toward our own imperfections, and maybe even learn to love them, we can improve our dancing. And this turns out to be just what we need to learn in order to deal with our perfectionism issues in other parts of our lives.

> The perfect is the enemy of the good.
>
> *Voltaire*

What would happen if we thought of perfection differently? What if, instead of thinking of perfection as inherently "right" or "best," we just thought of the impulse toward perfection as another habit leftover from an earlier part of our life? Perhaps one we don't need?

Breaking habits releases creativity and actually creates new anatomical structures in the brain. For fun, try some exercises to go beyond accepting imperfection—seek it and embrace it. Here are a few to try. We are sure you will think of others once you get the hang of it.

- Invite people over for dinner without having a perfectly clean and tidy house. Don't apologize for the imperfect condition of your home. See whether anyone reacts negatively to your piles of papers on the desk or somewhat dirty kitchen floor.
- Write a letter to a friend without spell-checking it. Make two errors and send it as is.
- Drive to the dance studio by the scenic route that takes longer and is less efficient. Enjoy the extra five or ten minutes "wasted" in the drive.
- When your dance partner makes an error, do not comment or appear to notice it.
- The next time your partner criticizes you, say, "Oh, thank you for pointing that out." Do this even if you are sure he or she is wrong.

What does this feel like? Does a shiver of fear run through you as you break the habit of perfection? Do these exercises exactly 40 times until you are perfectly imperfect ...oops!

Is the Coach Always Right?

> We protest against unjust criticism, but we accept unearned applause.
>
> *Jose Narosky*

OK, so we are working on learning to accept criticism. We are grappling with our resistance to change and our attachment to unrealistic perfectionism. All of this work on ourselves should help us become more open to the help our coach is trying to give us. The next logical question is whether we can trust this coach: Is the coach always right? The short answer is, yes, the coach is always right. Because our habits so often operate outside of our awareness we have to take on faith that what our coach tells us is more correct than our internal belief about what we are doing. We are reminded of something Pierre Allaire said to us in a coaching session.

No one at a competition knows what they are doing. The judges are moving to the music as they judge. They look like they wish they were dancing when they're supposed to be judging. The dancers are supposed to be dancing, but they are judging. A dancer will say, "How could that guy beat me!? I'm better than he is!" Really, how do you know? Were you judging? You were supposed to be dancing. And the audience—they are just supposed to be watching and enjoying the dancing, but they want to judge, too!

He's right. We tend to get caught up in judging ourselves. We have to remember—we're not qualified to judge! Just dance as well as you can at that moment in time and have fun doing it. Leave the judging to the judges, the teaching to the teachers, and your partner's half of the dance to your partner.

Body Awareness

Our ideas about what our bodies are doing are often wrong. Sometimes we respond to negative feedback with genuine surprise because we feel so sure that what we are doing is correct. This can be a sign that we have not understood the instruction properly, but it can also reflect our lack of knowledge about our own body. If you do something that feels to you like it matches what you are being told to do, but the coach says it is not, then you need to work on developing a better understanding of what is being asked of you. Often getting a certain image or idea about the movement will result in an "aha" experience of understanding that will then allow you to reliably reproduce it.

The opposite can also happen. You are being coached on a change, trying to make the change, and then you hear, "Yes, that's it!" and you think, "What? What did I do?" This is frustrating in a different way. If you weren't aware of what made it correct, you will not be able to reproduce it. In this case, what has to be developed is a heightened awareness of where your body is and what it is doing. Over time, as you get positive feedback, pay attention to what you were thinking and feeling, and try to reproduce that. Gradually, as you develop increased awareness, you will be able to do it on demand.

Remember the skill practice to develop body awareness in Chapter 8? Here is a more advanced version:

Skill Practice: Spatial Body Awareness, Gold Level

Looking straight ahead, stand with your feet 12 inches apart, toes parallel, facing forward. Line up your knees so they are straight. Now look down. Are your feet 12 inches apart? Are your feet and legs lined up as you thought, exactly parallel, or are they aligned differently?

Now, did your posture slump as you were distracted by your awareness of your feet? Correct your posture. How does that feel? Did you stop smiling? Add a smile, while keeping correct posture. How do you feel now? Do you feel confident that you can do this in front of your partner? Your teacher?

Try it again. Did you get the whole sequence of improvement this time?

Abusive Coaching

There are two exceptions to the "coach is always right" rule. One is when you just don't connect with a particular coach. Sometimes there are aspects of a coach's style and approach that make a particular coach not right *for you*. This doesn't mean that they are wrong, it just means you and that particular coach aren't a good fit. The chemistry is missing.

The abusive coach is a more serious problem. As we said in earlier chapters on respect, *do not work with anyone who is abusive.* Abuse in a relationship violates the respect rule. Remember that respect must be the foundation of all dance partnerships, including your partnership with your coach. Not only must you respect your coach, your coach must also treat you and your partner with respect, regardless of your dance level.

We must all take a great deal of what our coaches say on faith, because we do not have the ability to decide for ourselves whether the information we are getting is correct. That is why we pay a coach—for their superior knowledge and skill. This means we are investing our coach with a high level of trust and putting ourselves in a vulnerable position. It is impossible (and dangerous) to trust anyone who is abusive, and it is impossible to retain self-respect in the face of abuse. Regardless of reputation or credentials, if you are being abused, take responsibility for getting out of the relationship without delay. There are plenty of other well-qualified coaches out there who will treat you with respect and are fun to work with.

How do you know whether you are being abused? After all, you are paying the coach to criticize you and that may not feel very good. Some coaches are more tactful and others are more brusque in the way they give correction. The big difference between abusive and nonabusive critical feedback lies in whether the criticism is objective (focused on the dancing) or personal (focused on attacking you as a person). "We need to work on your head position," is about the dancing. "You look like a pig," is personal.

Abusive people try to enhance themselves by tearing others down. Good coaches speak with admiration about other coaches that they have learned from. They do not present themselves as the only bearers of truth.

Accepting Criticism Gracefully

> People ask for criticism, but they only want praise.
>
> *W. Somerset Maugham*

Maugham got it right: we ask for criticism, but we don't really want to hear it. Just as in our description of our first private lesson back in Chapter 8, when we dance for the coach, we are hoping to hear wild applause. At the same time, we realize that reverting to the six-year-old who just wants to be the teacher's pet and be "right" in front of everybody is pathetic and ridiculous. Then we get angry at ourselves for having those immature feelings. Meanwhile, all of this inner dialog about our emotional reaction to criticism is distracting us from paying attention to what the coach is trying to teach us—and then we get mad at ourselves about that. Whew!

Of course, this doesn't happen every time. Lots of times we are able to receive coaching gladly and gracefully, but then that inner six-year-old shows up without being invited. Sometimes the little brat is glad when it is our partner who gets the criticism—momentarily reinforcing the secret belief that, "the problem with my dancing is my partner." That illusion never lasts long...

Sometimes we do really well with criticism if we are the one bringing up the problem: "I would like help with X." In this instance, we know we are not dancing as well as we would like to and are openly searching for a better way to execute the technique.

Perhaps we are most crestfallen if we are criticized about a problem we thought we solved long ago, or something we think we are doing especially well.

The skill and tact of the coach are factors that can affect how difficult or easy it is to receive their critique, but it is important not to blame the coach for our reaction. Once we find a coach we like and trust, we need to stick with that person and believe in them. If you are never satisfied with *any* coach—perhaps it's not them, it just might be you.

As we pointed out in Chapter 5, our biological state has a big influence on our mood and learning, so in order to get the most benefit from expensive coaching it is wise to take responsibility for arriving at a coaching session physically and mentally prepared to learn. Be rested, hydrated, and fed so you are not distracted by your rumbling stomach, or feeling too tired to dance up to the level your coach is asking of you.

> Unless I accept my faults I will most certainly doubt my virtues.
>
> *Hugh Prather*

Perhaps the ultimate step in letting go of our perfectionism is accepting that sometimes we will *not* have a mature inner response to criticism. So when that inner six-year-old shows up and feels crushed about not being praised, instead of getting angry at our child-self we could just accept that this sometimes happens. We could try allowing ourselves to be a bit fond and amused, rather than harsh. What if we smiled an inner smile and said, "Hi. I see you're still in there."? Then we could just let it go and move on, instead of getting into a distracting cycle of self-blame. Maybe that will work.

And if it doesn't, maybe we can accept that as being OK, too.

> Whatever is in any way beautiful hath its source of beauty in itself, and is complete in itself; praise forms no part of it. So it is none the worse nor the better for being praised.
>
> *Marcus Aurelius Antoninus*

Review of Gold Level Responsibility: Accepting Criticism

Reasons we resist coaching
* Neophobia
* Fear of failure
* Habit

We cannot accept critique unless we let go of perfectionism

The coach is always right
* We need to increase body awareness
* Do not work with anyone who is abusive

Learn to accept criticism

Chapter 13

GOLD LEVEL RESPONSIVENESS: ACHIEVING SHARED FLOW

In Chapter 1 we described an experience of joyful dancing in the Sahara Desert. Why was it so easy to be spontaneous and joyful in our desert dance, we wondered, but so difficult to capture and hang on to that feeling of ecstatic abandon when we dance with a partner at home?

> **Shared joy is double joy; shared sorrow is half a sorrow.**
>
> **Swedish Proverb**

Throughout this book we have discussed in detail some of the major obstacles: the necessity of taking lessons to learn dance figures, with the inevitable development of expectations about executing them; self-consciousness; anxiety; perfectionism; and blame. We have talked about how dancing assaults our psychological defenses, surprising us by bringing out our unresolved issues, especially our "inner six-year-old."

If you, the reader, have been conscientious about applying the first two Rs, respect and responsibility, to your treatment of yourself, your partner, and your teacher, and have continued your study of dance with good coaches, you have become a more comfortable and confident dancer, more relaxed about being watched, and less anxious about what others may think of you. Like everyone, you still make mistakes, but you have learned not to live or die over them (at least, not as often…). You don't automatically blame your partner. You have, in fact, overcome the major obstacles to dancing with joy, and have had several tastes of "flow."

At this point in your dancing, the greatest challenge is the third R, responsiveness. This is because the coordination of movement between two people who are closely touching each other is inherently quite difficult, both physically and psychologically. Have you watched any of the popular dance shows on TV where people who are accomplished in jazz, tap, or ballet are required to learn ballroom dancing? They freak out! When someone is standing right in front of them, getting in their way, they can't move!

When you have been studying ballroom dancing for some time, it is easy to take this coordination for granted. We forget what it was like when we were first starting—worried about stepping on our partner, or wondering, "What should I do if she won't go?" All of that is in the past. If you can get down the floor with another person, execute recognizable dance figures in time to the music, look pretty good, and have a good time while doing it, you are doing amazingly well! This is a very difficult skill. Give yourself a pat on the back! But is having a good time the same as "flow?"

> I believe that the very purpose of our life is to seek happiness.
>
> *The Dalai Lama*

Cultivating Happiness

What is the proper place of happiness in our lives? Philosophers have puzzled over this question for centuries. Is happiness the same as pleasure? Is finding happiness the purpose of life, as the Dalai Lama says, or is seeking happiness sinful, as some religions have taught? Is a focus on personal happiness necessarily selfish, or are happy people actually more compassionate and kind than unhappy people?

Happiness and Pleasure

Life is filled with simple pleasures that can make us happy if we pay attention to them: the soothing sound of the wind blowing the leaves, the sight of sunlight glinting off the water, the scent of lilacs, the first taste of our morning coffee, the silky feel of a baby's skin, the miracle of the first spring shoots pushing up through the snow. But so often we ignore the beauty and wonder around us. We live "in our heads," reliving the past or planning for the future, but missing the present moment because we do not allow it into consciousness. Meditative practices to cultivate mindfulness train the practitioner to develop heightened awareness of "now." Another pathway to staying in the moment is through activities that require intense concentration.

At an earlier point in our lives we went whitewater rafting every summer with our adolescent and young adult children. In addition to the pleasure of finding a family vacation that adult children enjoyed, one of the great benefits of a rafting vacation was the intense concentration we experienced while shooting the rapids, which completely erased all thoughts of our everyday lives. On other vacations we had found it often took two or three days to really let go of "real life" back home and relax. On rafting trips, by contrast, we were in the present moment immediately and constantly.

Our early dance lessons surprised us by providing a similar "head vacation," one that we could take at home every week. We discovered that this intensity occurred mostly during private lessons, rather than during group lessons or social dancing. The mental and physical demands of a private lesson, with its focus on technique, called for being fully aware in the present moment, paying attention to very small cues. Just as in rafting the big rapids of the American West, we experienced total commitment of body and mind, which took us away from thoughts about whether the dishes had been washed or the mortgage paid. We had inadvertently discovered that studying dancing could be a form of meditation.

Flow

Psychologist Mihaly Csikszentmihalyi spent his career studying what he called "the psychology of optimal experience." He was interested in understanding what makes people happy, doing extensive research with thousands of people all over the world, from all walks of life. What he found was that happiness does not depend upon external events. Once people have the barest necessities, such as food and shelter, the conditions of life have very little to do with people's experience of happiness. Those who are rich, successful, and physically attractive are not necessarily happier than anyone else.

> The control of consciousness determines the quality of life.
>
> *Mihaly Csikszentmihalyi*

Regardless of culture, gender, or age, people who get the greatest enjoyment out of life are those who have learned to *focus their attention and direct their efforts to the goals they themselves have chosen.* These experiences, in turn, feed back into their sense of self, producing greater confidence.

A PBS series, "Frontier House," provided a striking illustration of this truth. Volunteer families were filmed in recreated conditions of homesteading in Montana in 1883. Parents and children worked hard all summer for basic food and shelter. When the series ended, the camera followed the families back into their modern lives. One of the children was shown wandering aimlessly through his expensive home, disconsolately playing video games, bored and depressed in the midst of riches. On the frontier he had been happily engaged in meaningful work caring for chickens to help his family survive. Useful, important work had clearly made him much happier than a passive experience of wealth.

Experiences of flow can occur any time we are deeply absorbed in what we are doing, but they most often occur when we are engrossed in an activity that makes high demands on skill—and we are able to meet those demands. At such moments we are fully concentrated, in harmony with our intention. The content of flow experiences varies from person to person: composing a piece of music, solving a mathematical problem, climbing a rock face. What they have in common is that they are experiences of great intensity. Arts and sports tend to be the pursuits in which flow is most likely to occur, although one can also achieve flow in work, especially in work that is challenging and meaningful.

Csikszentmihalyi concluded that:

happiness, in fact, is a condition that must be prepared for, cultivated, and defended privately by each person. People who learn to control inner experience will be able to determine the quality of their lives... (*Flow*, p. 4).

Therefore, we can create our own happiness through voluntary effort.

> The essence of all art is to have pleasure in giving pleasure.
>
> *Mikhail Baryshnikov*

Flow and Pleasure

Is flow the same as pleasure? Eating a delicious meal in good company, taking a refreshing nap, and sipping a cool drink while gazing with satisfaction on your freshly-mowed lawn are all pleasurable experiences, but they are not experiences of flow. And although it may sound as if taking drugs to get high might produce flow—"the state in which people are so involved in an activity that nothing else seems to matter; the experience itself is so enjoyable that people will do it even at great cost, for the sheer sake of doing it" (*Flow*, p. 4)—getting high does not result in flow, just short-term, pleasurable feelings. In fact, the passivity and diminished conscious awareness that characterize the experience of recreational drug use are the *opposite* of the active involvement and intensified consciousness that are the hallmarks of flow.

Flow occurs:

...when a person's skills are fully involved in overcoming a challenge that is just about manageable. Optimal experiences usually involve a fine balance between one's ability to act and the available opportunities for action... When high challenges are matched with high skills, then the deep involvement that sets flow apart from ordinary life is likely to occur (*Flow*, p. 30).

Interestingly, activities that people later describe as experiences of "flow," are not necessarily very pleasurable while they are occurring. In moments of flow, the person's consciousness is so fully concentrated in the present moment that there is no attentional capacity left over for evaluating the quality of the experience. All consciousness is being used *in* the experience. It is only in looking back on it that people realize they were in flow. Over time,

> ...optimal experiences add up to a sense of mastery—or perhaps better, a sense of participation in determining the content of life—that comes as close to what is usually meant by happiness as anything else we can conceivably imagine (*Flow*, p. 4).

This is the experience that athletes have described as being "in the zone," and Zen masters call "satori." When we are in flow, time seems to slow down, and it is common for people to report feelings of heightened sensory awareness, ecstasy, and feelings of "oneness" with the experience.

Sports psychologist Terry Orlick describes such an experience:

One winter night, the sky was clear, the moon was full, the night air crisp. The snow sparkled like dancing crystals under the moonlight... As I skied down, I became one with the mountain, not knowing where it ended and where I started. I was so close to it, hugging it, it hugging me, as I flowed along that tiny, snow-packed trail... I was totally absorbed in the experience... it was novel, challenging, sensual, fun, exciting, physically demanding, a meaningful experience with nature... a peak experience, the kind that makes it great to be alive (*In Pursuit of Excellence*, p. 12).

As a freely chosen activity that, at its best, presents high levels of challenge and places great demands upon skill, dancing is a perfect activity for producing flow experiences. Once we have this experience, we keep trying to re-create it. And when flow occurs together with a partner, it is truly an addictive experience, in the best, healthy sense of the word.

Technique—the Pathway to Flow

You didn't think we were going to start talking about technique at this point, did you? The problem is, most of us are introduced to technique as something arbitrary that someone wants us to do for no obvious reason. Initially, we view it as something we have to put up with, or something "the judges want to see." What we don't understand until much later is that dance technique is the means by which some incredibly smart people, sometime, somewhere, figured out the physics of how to make partnered dancing work.

It is hard to realize that the details of technique are not only helpful, they are absolutely necessary. "Heel-toe, toe, toe-heel"—what is it for? We conceptualize points of technique as hurdles that are always a "test," rather than understanding that correct technique is what allows us to move down the floor as a team, two bodies flowing together as one with the music and each other. It is correct technique that enables us to move subtly out of each other's way as we execute the dance figures.

Proper head position, for example, is vital to a spin turn or pivot. If either partner's head falls toward their shared center, the centripetal force will prevent the couple from moving down the floor, and the other partner will feel "blocked." When both heads stay on the outside of the circle, each partner feels freer, and the couple can move easily as one. Correct footwork and body shaping allow the gentleman to send signals to the lady about changes in direction and timing so that her "follow," only a split second later, feels and appears seamless. Technique is designed to provide the maximum opportunity for responsiveness in the partnership.

The dance figures themselves also have a purpose—doing a whisk or a twinkle, for example, will allow us to change direction while continuing to move in time to the music. Every dance figure has been designed to achieve some aim within the language of the dance.

The ritual of wine service is analogous. Each part of the "show" is designed to achieve certain aims: first the bottle is displayed—this allows you to verify that this bottle is actually the wine you ordered, including the correct year. A chilled wine is wrapped in a cloth so the warmth of the server's hand will not affect the temperature of the wine. The cork is removed in front of you, verifying that a different wine has not been substituted in the kitchen. The cork is presented so that you can check it for soundness and mold. A small amount of wine is then poured with the bottle not touching the rim of the glass, so that the outside of the bottle, which might have dust or cobwebs from being cellared, doesn't dirty the glass that will touch your lips. The server leaves the glass on the table or a tray during pouring, so that their hand doesn't soil the glass.

You swirl the wine in the glass to release the bouquet, sniff, then sip. If you approve the wine's taste, it will then be served, first to your guests, and last to you, the host. Each part of this ritual has a reason, rooted in the days when a much higher percentage of bottles were spoiled and undrinkable, and the year made a big difference in the quality of a wine. Each part of the wine service has a practical, historical reason designed to solve the problem of how to get you the wine you ordered in a clean glass.

Later, it became a ritual, part of the pleasurable experience of being served a bottle of wine. Nowadays, people who are unfamiliar with the origins of this ritual may view it as pretentious or even stupid. Dance technique is like this. If you don't understand why you are doing it, that doesn't make it stupid or arbitrary—it may be that you do not yet understand why it is actually helping you achieve your objective.

Technique Is Your Friend

Technique, though important at every level of dancing, becomes increasingly important at higher levels, because higher level figures actually cannot be executed without proper technique. The bodies are too close, the rotation is too great, and the changes of direction and position are too fast. Without proper technique, higher level moves just don't work.

Correct dance technique produces efficient movement. We get farther down the floor with less effort. A simple example is the shift from bronze to silver—passing your feet allows you to move with less effort over a distance. And correct technique enables partners to dance together with full body contact, even in dances as fast as the quickstep. Correct technique fosters responsiveness in the partnership.

In Chapter 11 we proposed a new adage for dancers, "Reality is your friend." A corollary is, "Technique is your friend." Does this sound crazy? Nearly everyone regards technique as the enemy, a dragon to be slain. Even if it is taught as a useful tool (which it usually is not), the truth that technique is your friend seems unbelievable until you have achieved a rather sophisticated understanding of dance. Children undoubtedly have an advantage here. Proper technique probably doesn't seem any more arbitrary to them than hundreds of other things grownups tell them are important, like brushing their teeth, making their beds, and learning subtraction.

> How can you think and hit at the same time?
>
> *Yogi Berra*

Technique as Meditation

Once we understand that any activity that requires intense concentration forces us to stay in the moment, it becomes clear that any activity in which we engage with intensity can, potentially, bring us into a state of flow. This is the basis of the Zen approach to studying the arts. As D. T. Suzuki explains in the introduction to Herrigel's *Zen in the Art of Archery*,

> ...all the arts as they are studied in Japan... are not intended for utilitarian purposes only or for purely aesthetic enjoyments, but are meant to train the mind; indeed, to bring it into contact with the ultimate reality... the swordsman does not wield the sword just for the sake of outdoing his opponent; the dancer does not dance just to perform certain rhythmical movements of the body. The mind has first to be attuned to the Unconscious. If one really wishes to be master of an art, technical knowledge of it is not enough. One has to transcend technique so that the art becomes an "artless art" growing out of the Unconscious (pp. v–vi).

This approach shifts the focus from outcome to process. The study of any art, including the martial arts, flower arranging, or dancing, then becomes a vehicle for spiritual growth. Learning the correct execution of a pivot, improving our body position in a cross-body lead, and studying proper foot placement in a cross-over break are no longer ends in themselves. They are all exercises through which, by practice and study, we are eventually able to experience a "letting go," an effortlessness that comes only from disciplined repetition. Through this "letting go," the "artless art" is transformed into "art."

> Master technique and then forget about it and be natural.
>
> *Anna Pavlova*

There is a paradox here. Technique is studied, practiced, and repeated so that it may be transcended. In dancing we speak of practicing until correct technique is in "muscle memory." When a movement is in muscle memory, its production is actually coming from a different part of the brain than it is when we are first learning it, like "automatically" driving your car. When correct technique is automatic, we can release our awareness of it and focus on other aspects of the dance, such as floor craft and partnership—but we can successfully transcend technique only if our muscle memory produces it correctly and reliably.

By rethinking what practicing technique means, we can transform our attitude. Instead of "boring-old-technique," repetitive practice becomes a meditation to learn to stay in the moment, embrace reality, and focus.

Technique and the Partnership

All partnered activities present a unique challenge: We are responsible for ourselves, but we also depend on our partner. If we do not compress and release together, if our centers do not communicate, if either of us has a frame that is too stiff or too soft, we cannot produce the dance at the highest level. In partnered dancing, we can't get the experience of flow by ourselves. Our partner must do his or her part.

Though the moments of shared flow are brief, when they are suddenly interrupted, we may react like an addict whose drug was just snatched away—with intense negativity that makes no "objective" sense. Higher level partnership produces more flow, but this, in turn, creates more opportunities for loss of flow. The challenge, thus, is to manage this sudden transition in such a way that we continually build and repair, rather than damage the partnership.

Such moments are much less jarring and easier to manage without negative emotion if we have been consistently practicing the **3 Rs**. If we have learned to radically accept reality, respecting ourselves and our partner, and releasing the habit of blame, we may be able to meet the sudden loss of flow calmly, breathing and smiling. Calm acceptance of such an interruption helps to keep it brief, facilitating a smooth return to a positive shared dance experience.

> There are short-cuts to happiness, and dancing is one of them.
>
> *Vicki Baum*

Perfectionism and Flow

Oh, no! Not perfectionism again!

Oh, yes.

We perfectionists can create anxiety about anything—even about whether we are experiencing the "right" kind of happiness. Is *this* flow? How about *this*?

Obviously, the moment you begin to worry about whether you are in flow, you aren't, even if you were. The hallmark of flow is complete absorption in what you are doing. Anxiety automatically brings about a division of attention. You stop concentrating on what you are doing and begin self-evaluating. Anxiety about how you are performing is actually a tremendous distraction. Learning to focus and concentrate means letting go of all self-evaluation. You really can't self-evaluate. You're not qualified.

So cut that out! Who cares if you are in flow! Just go out there, focus on what you are doing, and have a good time. Live it, without worrying about whether you are having the "right" or "best" kind of pleasure.

Happiness and Relationships

We have been discussing flow as if it were the only path to happiness. But we must not overlook the fact that relationships with other people are also a major source of human happiness. Although some people are more introverted, and some are more extroverted, we are a social species. Most of us would not be happy as hermits. As psychoanalyst John Bowlby, one of the pioneers of attachment theory, put it:

> Intimate attachments to other human beings are the hub around which a person's life revolves, not only when he is an infant or a toddler or a schoolchild but throughout his adolescence and his years of maturity as well, and on into old age. From these intimate attachments a person draws his strength and enjoyment of life and, through what he contributes, he gives strength and enjoyment to others (*Loss*, p. 442).

Partnership is all about attachment. So when we are flowing along having a wonderful time, and that flow is suddenly interrupted because of something we think our partner has done, we must remain aware of the value we place on the partnership. We can't do ballroom dancing by ourselves; so we must remember, "It's not all about me."

> Kindness is more important than wisdom, and the recognition of this is the beginning of wisdom.
>
> *Theodore Rubin*

Kindness and Compassion

We need each other. Sometimes we wish we didn't, but we do. After all, this whole book is about how to preserve your relationship with your partner and still enjoy dancing together. In that moment when our flow is suddenly interrupted, we feel startled; there is a sudden shift in attention and mood. And then it is easy to snap at our partner. Sometimes we will still do this, no matter how much we study the **3Rs**.

At these times try to cultivate kindness and compassion. These qualities are valuable, not only in the dance partnership, but in life. If everyone in the world conscientiously cultivated kindness and compassion we would see an end to discrimination, cruelty, and war. We would have heaven on earth. We are realistic enough to know that we are unlikely to see this happen in our lifetime, but we can still "tend our own garden" and try to make the small space we occupy on earth a little better by the way we treat ourselves and others.

How can we learn to be more compassionate? First, if we have the intention to develop compassion, we will immediately be in a different, more positive, frame of mind. (Yes, happy people are more kind and compassionate.) This mindset, in turn, helps us slow down the speed of our response when we feel something negative toward ourselves or another person. The habit of negative judging is usually quite automatic. Inserting a pause before speaking negatively (internally or externally) can give us the extra time we need to challenge our negative thinking. We are all human beings. Everyone does what they do for a reason. If we can develop a habit of empathy, we feel kinder. We become curious about behavior: I wonder why he is doing that? I wonder what it feels like to live her life?

When we feel negatively toward someone else, a compassionate internal response could be to think either that we must have misunderstood something (due to inadequate communication or incomplete information), or that anxiety (ours or theirs) underlies the problem. Without going too deeply into the complexities of human behavior, simply imagining that there is probably a legitimate explanation that would change our reaction can be enormously helpful in making us more patient and forbearing. (Caveat: This does not include allowing yourself to be abused.)

So when your flow is interrupted by a loss of mutual attunement, be forgiving, have compassion, and get back to focusing on the dancing. If a big discussion is not needed, don't go there. Just say, "I guess we should try that again." Return to what you were doing, tune in to each other, and refocus on moving responsively. Let it go, and dance the board you are on. You will soon return to a positive shared experience. Of course, if this happens repeatedly in the same spot, use the *Rule of Three*, and take it to your teacher.

A non-dancing experience showed us clearly just how much we had developed our mutual responsiveness. During a cleaning spree we decided to surprise Betty's mother with a new rug in her bedroom. Inviting her to take a nap in the next room while we cleaned, we silently moved all the furniture out of her room, took out the old rug, and replaced it during her nap. We were able to coordinate our movements without speaking (Betty's mother is a light sleeper), and without bumping the furniture into the walls or doorway, because of our extensive practice of being attuned to each other's movement through dancing. We gave and received a lot of pleasure as we worked together in coordinated harmony.

Once again, our study of partnered dancing can become an opportunity for personal growth. And isn't that really why we are doing it? Sometimes our non-dancing friends will ask us what we win when we compete, and we laugh. Our "prize" is a ribbon or a medal or a trophy, but the real prize is the learning. We learn about our bodies. We learn about our feelings and thoughts and memories. We learn about ourselves and about each other. And, with patience, work, and the **3 Rs**, we can learn to deepen our partnership off, as well as on the dance floor.

> When I dance, I cannot judge, I cannot hate, I cannot separate myself from life. I can only be joyful and whole, that is why I dance.
>
> *Hans Bos*

Review of Gold Level Responsiveness: Achieving Shared Flow

We all seek happiness
* Some happiness comes from simple pleasure
* Some happiness comes from flow

Finding flow

- Flow occurs when high challenge meets high skill
- In ballroom dancing we need our partner to find flow
- Flow occurs at high levels of responsiveness

Technique is the pathway to flow

- Studying technique can be a form of meditation

Perfectionism impedes flow

Cultivating kindness and compassion in relationships increases happiness

Chapter 14

BEYOND THE DANCE: APPLYING RELATIONSHIP SKILLS IN LIFE

> We're fools whether we dance or not, so we might as well dance.
>
> *Japanese Proverb*

Summing Up: So what have we tried to learn from dancing?

Dancing is often used by writers and psychologists as a metaphor for repetitive patterns of behavior in relationships. (See, for example, Lerner's *The Dance of Anger*.) Recurring patterns in a couple's relationship off the dance floor *do*, in fact, make their way onto the dance floor. It was our observation of these interactions in group classes that first piqued our interest as psychologists. We quickly recognized issues familiar to us from our clinical work: desire for and fear of intimacy; shame and blame; dominance and submission; trust and anxiety; sensuality and inhibition; jealousy and kindness; tenderness and anger—it was all there in front of us. And—we experienced the power of dancing first hand, to challenge and change our own relationship.

When dancing together exposes a relationship issue, the couple faces a choice that will have major implications for the future of their relationship. If they choose to ignore it, pretending it is invisible, they run the risk of eventually either changing partners or giving up dancing. If they decide to notice it, their choices expand: they can blame each other, sulk, change teachers, or change themselves and their relationship. Making the last of these choices feels the most risky, but the payoff can be huge: a deeper and stronger relationship both on and off the dance floor.

When we made the decision to take dance lessons we had no idea we were embarking on a journey of self-discovery and "play therapy" for our marriage. (We actually thought it would be a cheap hobby. Buy a pair of dance shoes, take a few lessons, and you're home free...)

There were times when we seriously considered giving up dancing—it would have been easier than changing ourselves or our relationship (or continually hearing about keeping our head to the left!). Having stuck it out for 15 years, through different teachers and coaches, the constant has been our commitment to our marriage and our fundamental belief that a good relationship is strengthened by noticing, discussing, and working to solve problems, rather than ignoring them. It takes courage and faith. It's not easy. But, ultimately, it is worth it— the marriage is more fun.

> You gain strength, courage, and confidence by every experience in which you really stop to look fear in the face. You must do the thing which you think you cannot do.
>
> *Eleanor Roosevelt*

Courage

Does it seem strange to be talking about courage? You recall that way back in Chapter 1 when we introduced the problem that led us to write this book, we said that dancing assaults our psychological defenses. Why do we need defenses?

We construct defenses to oversimplify our world and protect us from the pain of seeing something within us we don't like.

When we might feel embarrassed, ashamed, or guilty, our defenses may protect us from pain. But we have another choice. We can look at whatever we don't like about ourselves without excuse, explanation, or blame. And then we can decide to do something about it: Accept it, change it, or change our feelings about it. To decide to change is a huge act of courage.

> Yes, risk taking is inherently failure-prone. Otherwise, it would be called sure-thing-taking.
>
> *Tim McMahon*

The strange thing about finally talking honestly about issues that make us uncomfortable is that we are always surprised that what happens is not as bad as we feared it would be. The more we face our feelings, the more we grow. But it takes courage every time. And when our world doesn't fall apart, after all, we feel tremendous relief. Most amazing of all, when we confront problems honestly and work on them together we find that, not only do we feel wonderful afterward, the solutions we create are unexpected—ones we could not have envisioned when we began.

Dancing turns out to be a wonderful activity for helping us develop courage and confidence. It does assault our defenses, therefore, it presents many opportunities for growth. The repetitive nature of dance guarantees that we will encounter same issues over and over. If we keep seeing the same problem in the same context, with the same result, how long can we ignore it? (Sometimes for a long time.)

Any partnered activity offers the opportunity to challenge a relationship. (Like writing a book together...) When we told a friend about the psychological issues that led us to write this book, she said, "Oh, I know what you're talking about. I used to play doubles tennis with my husband, but we gave up. Even when the coach kept telling him to stay on his own side he just couldn't trust me to take the shots that were my responsibility. He had to play on his side of the court and mine, too. After awhile, we gave up trying to play doubles as a team."

Sound familiar? For most couples it is easier to change their hobby than their relationship.

Changing partners is a common pattern among pros. Apparently, many of them feel it's easier to dissolve their partnership, even a championship partnership, than to solve their relationship problems. And maybe that works for their dancing. But does it work for their life?

> With courage you will dare to take risks, have the strength to be compassionate, and the wisdom to be humble. Courage is the foundation of integrity.
>
> *Keshavan Nair*

Faith

We are not talking about religious faith here, although if you are religious, your faith may help you. We are speaking here of *faith in the process*. Faith makes courage possible. With faith in the process, you can trust that it will lead you to the outcome that will be right for you. Too often we become attached to a particular answer to a problem, and try to force the process toward that "solution." It takes courage and faith to let go of what you "know" will work, and allow the process to unfold organically. If you believe and practice this, you may be surprised at the unexpected and creative outcomes that will emerge naturally.

As psychologists, we were fortunate to have the training and experience that gave us the tools to work on the relationship issues that were uncovered by our dancing together. We certainly didn't have any "magic" that would make it automatic, easy or painless. What we did have was faith that if we "hung in there" together long enough, we could work through (and rework) each issue as it arose. In this book we have tried to share with you the principles and the tools that we found most useful for us in our dancing, and in our life. As we review them here, use dance as a metaphor. Think about how each principle applies to your life beyond the dance.

The Three Rs

Respect (Chapters 2, 6, 7, 10, and 11)

Respect is the foundation of any positive relationship. Respect yourself, your partner, and your teacher. Keep an open mind and apply the **Rule of Three** as needed during practice. Respect other dancers. Respect the difficulty of the activity. Respect reality. You will never be perfect.

Behave so that you can respect yourself. Choose partners, teachers, and coaches not only for their dance abilities, but for what they are like as people. You will be spending a lot of time with them; some of it intense. You want to be in the company of people you can respect as human beings. Steer clear of people who are disrespectful, and especially, those who are abusive.

This doesn't mean that you can't kid around and have fun. Dancing should be fun. But beware of humor that might hurt people's feelings. The witty remark can cut deeply. Kindness trumps cleverness every time.

Don't confuse dance with romance. Be true to yourself and your values. Proper technique is your guide to appropriate violation of personal space. Learn what to do and what not to do within the framework of the dance.

Embrace and love reality. It is only when we accept reality that we can begin to change. Be aware that your version of reality and your partner's version of reality are different—and that doesn't mean that either one of you is wrong! You are separate people. You are having different experiences, even when you are in the same place at the same time.

Use "I-Messages." When you speak sincerely about your own experience, no one can tell you that you are wrong. You feel what you feel.

Express what you feel, but be interested in your partner's experience. Really listen when your partner is speaking, rather than preparing your response. A sincere interest in another person's experience can lead to a shift in the interaction. Respect is good for relationships.

When you are angry, hurt, or anxious, be especially vigilant about treating yourself and others with respect. Breathe and think before speaking. Slow down. Take a break. Go to the restroom. Drink water.

When you do, inevitably, make mistakes and hurt people, stop. Apologize and make amends. If you often say mean things to yourself, challenge that habit and change it. Be kind to yourself. Don't demand or expect perfection from yourself or others. Expect and accept mistakes. Forgive yourself and others. Make mutual respect the foundation of every interaction.

Responsibility (Chapters 3, 5, 6, 8, 10, and 12)

In life and in dance, take responsibility for your own behavior. Stay over your own feet and on your own side literally, and metaphorically. Dance your own part, but *only* your part. Allow your partner to dance—remember, in dance and in life,

"He goes, she goes,"—you don't get to take all the turns. Be generous with sincere compliments. Don't be too "helpful"—it can be distracting and annoying. You can cripple a butterfly by "helping" it emerge from its chrysalis. Let the teacher teach.

Avoid blaming: your partner, your teacher, or the floor. Blame is not only the enemy of partnership, it is the enemy of change.

Be prepared, mentally and physically. You might need to do fitness training, change your diet, get enough sleep, buy a pair of dance shoes, drink more water, learn to be on time, change your attitude, learn manners, or practice on your own. Whatever it is, take responsibility for figuring it out, then do what *you* need to do to be ready to dance. (And to live.) Use your values to guide your choices. Don't expect to "get it right" every time, but hang in there and keep trying.

Once you have found a teacher/coach you trust, listen to their advice and try to follow it. Don't waste their time and your money arguing with them. Open yourself to correction, feedback, and criticism. Be eager to learn. Accepting coaching can be painful, but it is the shortest route to improvement, and it is wonderful mental discipline.

Don't be too humble or too proud. You are neither as bad as you fear nor as great as you imagine. The reality lies somewhere in-between. Take responsibility for doing the best you can at any particular moment in time, while knowing it can always be better. Dedicate yourself to improvement, not perfection. Perfection is an illusion. Perfectionism is a trap that interferes with focus and guarantees disappointment. If perfection is the only thing that can make you happy, you are destined to be unhappy. Take charge of your own happiness.

Develop a fascination with learning how to learn. Enjoy the process. Be patient with yourself and your partner. Beware of neophobia. Learn to change old habits. Control that inner six-year-old.

Don't try to judge yourself; you're not qualified.

Practice, practice, practice.

> Nobody cares if you can't dance well. Just get up and dance.
>
> **Dave Barry**

Responsiveness (Chapters 4, 6, 9, 10, and 13)

Don't get hung up on or intimidated by the idea of "leading and following." In a responsive partnership the lead passes back and forth. It doesn't matter who is "in charge." You are each in charge of yourself. In life, leading and following are both skills we need—we can't have one without the other. Neither is inherently more valuable than the other. Develop flexibility in attitude, as well as in body.

Dancing can help you learn to develop power and use it wisely. Learn to be powerful within yourself. Don't try to impose yourself on others. If you are strong and powerful, your partner will be happy to learn how to join with you, just as you, in turn, strive to match your powerful partner.

Use dancing to help you learn to "tune in" to others. Try to feel what is happening. Have an intention of openness toward your partner. Be trustworthy and develop trust in your partner. Attunement and trust will make your partnership stronger both on and off the floor.

If you experience a failure of responsiveness from your partner, try to tune in to what is happening, instead of getting angry. An angry attack leads to a defensive response. Then you have two problems to solve. Be gently inquisitive about what is happening. Listen without the mindset that you already have the "right" answer. When being "right" begins to feel important, ask yourself, "Do I want to be right, or do I want to be happy?"

Distraction (external or internal) is the most common cause of responsiveness failure. If your partner is not tuning in to you, it is almost certainly not personal. Their focus is simply elsewhere.

Use dancing as a mental discipline—a form of meditation.

Your positive intention to be responsive to your partner will reap great dividends in the relationship. It will also help you develop patience, kindness, and compassion. A story is told that the Dalai Lama refused to fire his incompetent cook because he believed it would help him develop patience and acceptance. Turn problems into developmental challenges for yourself.

Have a positive intention to be happy. Appreciate your wonderful life. Be amazed at what you have accomplished. Be grateful that you don't live in thirteenth-century Europe, or in a hovel with a dirt floor and nothing to eat. A friend says that when her uncle wakes up every day, before he opens his eyes he pushes his elbows out to the side: "If I don't feel wood, it's a good day!" What a great attitude! He is aging with a sense of humor. Take that attitude onto the dance floor and into your life. Dance with joy.

> Life engenders life. Energy creates energy. It is by spending oneself that one becomes rich.
>
> *Sarah Bernhardt*

Centering and Balance

In dancing we are always searching for balance. We are constantly aware of our center, our partner's center, and our shared center. When we dance through our centers, we are balanced. This looks and feels good. Of course, we could have balance easily—just stand still and do nothing—but then there would be no dancing, and no joy.

Centering and balance are also fundamental concepts in life. When we are mentally centered we feel harmonious within ourselves. Our beliefs and values are consistent with our actions. We feel good about ourselves. But when we are in relationship with others we must also accommodate to their beliefs, values, and desires. We could live alone, but then we would be missing out on relationships—which give meaning to our lives.

Most of us are constantly searching for balance in our lives. There are so many things that request or demand our attention. Shall I do this or this? Each is worthy. Each is consistent with my values. But every choice entails a loss. If I do this, I cannot also do that. Time is the ultimate scarce resource. How shall I allocate my limited self? If I sat in my room and did nothing, I wouldn't make a mistake, but then I wouldn't really be living, just existing.

> Besides the noble art of getting things done, there is the noble art of leaving things undone. The wisdom of life consists in the elimination of non-essentials.
>
> *Lin Yutang*

Asking ourselves why we dance can help us find the proper place of dance in our lives. After all, there are other things in life that we value. If, for example, we spend so much money on dancing that we have none left over to give to charitable causes we believe in, then our life is probably out of balance. Here are some of the reasons *we* dance that feel right to us. You may have different reasons that are right for *you*.

Shared Enjoyment

This is all we bargained for when we first decided to take dance lessons. We thought it would be fun—a way to spend time together, a date for an hour once a week. When our youngest child finished high school and left home, we had more free time and energy to pay attention to our couple relationship, and dancing became our "empty nest" hobby. A great deal of research supports the idea that spending time together in a pleasurable activity strengthens couple relationships. Fun, it turns out, is good for you!

We have made many new, compatible friends from all over the country through competitive dancing.

And sometimes we even get a taste of "flow."

Health

Through dancing we became interested in strength training, cardiovascular fitness, and stretching. We began to fight actively against the toll time was taking on our aging bodies. We can truly say we are in better shape now than we were 15 years ago. This allows us to move through the activities of our everyday lives with more power, stamina, and confidence.

Dancing even saved Art from a heart attack. Here's how Betty recalls what happened: We had already been dancing for several years. We were practicing the quickstep on our own and had just danced the first two lines. We were coming to the end of the short side when I felt Art slowing down. "Come on, keep up!" I said. "You're slowing down." "I know," he replied. "I'm out of breath. I've got to get back the gym."

(A couple of months earlier Art had stopped going to work out on his doctor's advice after he had pneumonia.) Soon after our quickstep practice, Art phoned the fitness trainer to make an appointment. "I can't see you without your doctor's clearance," the trainer said. So Art made a doctor's appointment. His physician ordered a stress test, which he flunked. The next day he had a cardiac catheterization that showed over 90 percent blockage in three major coronary arteries, and 80 percent blockage in a fourth. He was immediately scheduled for a quadruple coronary bypass.

As we were walking the halls of the hospital awaiting surgery, the cardiologist cautioned him to slow down: "You are a heart attack waiting to happen," he said. It was hard to believe we had been dancing the quickstep only a short time before, and now he was being told walking might be too strenuous! The doctors later told him that the collateral vessels his body had grown to meet the demands of the sustained exercise of dancing had saved his life. Now his physician checks at every visit; "Are you still dancing?"

Research has shown that not only is ballroom dancing one of the best activities for cardiovascular fitness, it is also one of the few activities associated with a lower risk of dementia. In addition, we often find that the enhanced body awareness, strength, and balance we have developed through dancing helps shield us from injury or falls, and even enables us to change direction quickly. One time we were taking a walk when a pickup truck suddenly pulled forward out of a driveway. (The driver, busy on a cell phone, was oblivious to pedestrians.) We jumped back just in time to avoid being hit, looked at each other and said, "Thank you, dancing!"

Personal Growth and Relationship Development

The opportunity to use dance as a vehicle for personal growth has been the most unexpected bonus from our dancing. And even after all the time we have put in, we can always learn more about ourselves and our partnership. Through this book we have tried to share some of that learning with you.

But now our time together is coming to a close. We know that this book is not perfect, but we have learned to be more comfortable with imperfection. We have done our best to share some ideas and tools we found useful in our struggle to improve ourselves and our partnership in dancing and in our life together. We hope they may prove useful to you as you embark on your own personal quest. Now it is your turn.

> If I am not for myself, who will be for me? If I am only for myself what am I? And if not now, when?
>
> *Rabbi Hillel*

REFERENCES

Bowlby, J. 1980. *Attachment and Loss.* Volume III: Loss. New York: Basic Books.

Brill, P. W. 2003. *The Core Program.* New York: Bantam Books.

Csikszentmihalyi, M. 1990. *Flow: The Psychology of Optimal Experience.* New York: Harper & Row.

Duyff, R. L. 1998. *The American Dietetic Association's Complete Food and Nutrition Guide.* Minneapolis, Minn.: Chronimed Publishing.

Gordon, T. 2000 *Parent Effectiveness Training.* New York: Three Rivers Press.

Herrigel, E. 1953. *Zen in the Art of Archery.* New York: Pantheon Books.

Lerner, H. G. 1985. *The Dance of Anger.* New York: Harper & Row.

Mattes, A. L. 2000. *Active Isolated Stretching.* Sarasota, Fla.: Aaron L. Mattes.

Millman, D. 1999. *Body Mind Mastery.* Novato, Cal.: New World Library.

Orlick, T. 2000. *In Pursuit of Excellence.* Champaign, Ill.: Human Kinetics.

Stephenson, R. M., and J. Iaccarino. 1980. *The Complete Book of Ballroom Dancing*. New York: Doubleday.

Taylor, S. E. 1991. *Positive Illusions: Creative Self-Deception and the Healthy Mind*. New York: Basic Books.

Yelon, S. L. 1996. *Powerful Principles of Instruction*. White Plains, N.Y.: Longman Publishers.

PARTNER COMPATIBILITY QUESTIONNAIRE

Feel free to make copies of this page. Have each member of the prospective partnership complete it, circling or filling in answers as appropriate, and then discuss the results together to help you decide if you are potentially compatible as dance partners. You will get a preview of the relationship not only from the content of the answers you each give, but also from what the discussion feels like.

1. What style(s) of dance do you want to do?

   ❐ American Smooth   ❐ Swing

   ❐ American Rhythm   ❐ Country

   ❐ International Standard   ❐ Salsa

   ❐ International Latin   ❐ Hustle

2. Do you want a partner for dancing:

   ❐ Socially

   ❐ Competitively

   ❐ Both

3. What is your current proficiency level?

   ❐ Bronze   ❐ Gold

   ❐ Silver   ❐ Advanced

4. How much time per week would you like to commit to:

   ❐ Lessons/coaching

   ❐ Practice

   ❐ Social dancing

5. How do you anticipate cost-sharing?

    ☐ Half-and-half   ☐ Some other way (What?)

    _____

    (Note that for competitive dancing, detailed discussion of cost is needed because package costs differ for shared vs. non-shared rooms, travel may not be together, and costume costs are typically higher for the lady.)

6. What personal qualities are you looking for in a dance partner?

    _____

    _____

7. Do you use:
    ☐ Tobacco
    ☐ Alcohol
    ☐ Recreational drugs

8. Would you be open to a social relationship beyond the dance partnership?

    ☐ Yes, possibly.   ☐ No, I am gay.

    ☐ Probably not.   ☐ No, I think it is unwise to socialize with a dance partner.

    ☐ No, I am already   ☐ No, no reason.
      in a committed
      relationship.

9. Are you willing to follow the principles in this book and establish a partnership based upon mutual respect, individual responsibility, and interpersonal responsiveness?

   ☐ Yes   ☐ No

10. How would you solve a disagreement during a practice?

   _____

   _____

11. Have you had previous partners? What happened to the partnership(s)?

   _____

   _____

12. Are there other issues we should discuss? What?

   _____

   _____

Additional questions for competitive dancers:

13. How many competitions do you want to do a year?

   _____

14. How much are you able/willing to travel to competitions?

   _____

   _____

15. Coaching: Who is coaching you now?

_____

_____

Do you want to continue with him/her?

☐ Yes   ☐   No

Are you open to using other coaches?

☐ Yes   ☐   No

SOME BASIC PRINCIPLES OF HUMAN LEARNING AS APPLIED TO TEACHING DANCE

1. *Provide a pleasant learning environment.* This applies to both the physical and the interpersonal aspects of the environment.

Physical: The dance studio should be clean and well-lighted. Décor need not be elaborate or expensive, but it should be esthetically pleasing. Bathrooms should be clean and appropriately supplied. Space should be provided for dancers to hang coats or leave wet boots and umbrellas. A changing room should be provided for dancers who want to change out of street clothing into practice outfits. The need for appropriate flooring and music is self evident. The overall impression should be both welcoming and professional.

Interpersonal: Teachers should be clean and neatly dressed. They should greet dancers with a smile and eye contact when they enter the studio and introduce students to each other. Instructors should present material with enthusiasm. They should believe and project the attitude that dancing is fun. Teaching should be friendly and supportive in tone, even when mistakes are being corrected. For example, "That's good, you've almost got it, you just need to shift your weight a bit sooner," not, "That looks terrible!" Avoid comparing one dancer to another to the detriment of either. Criticism should always be about the dancing, not the student. "Bring your feet together on two," not, "You are so sloppy!"

2. *Find out what students want and expect.* You can be doing a great job of teaching the waltz, but if the students want to learn the cha cha, they will be dissatisfied. Similarly, if they only want to learn a lot of patterns, and you want to improve their technique, they

may be unhappy. Initiate conversations about students' desires and seek feedback about whether the instruction is meeting their needs.

3. *Find out what students already know.* This means not just whether they can do the rumba, but whether they have foundational skills for what you plan to teach. For example, we often hear the instruction to "change weight." Students need to know what you mean by basic instructions such as this. If they don't, you need to teach the foundational skill first, before teaching a pattern that requires this knowledge. Review is a powerful diagnostic tool for you, as well as an instructional tool for students.

4. *Define your terms.* Instructional vocabulary is a very confusing aspect of dance teaching because of the different names used by the Arthur Murray, Fred Astaire, and Independent studios. American and International styles also have different names for the same movements and different ways of doing dances that have the same names, which greatly adds to the confusion of the learner. Make sure you explain and show what you mean by different terms you plan to use in teaching. Check to see if students understand your explanations. Always demonstrate what you mean by dancing it.

5. *Involve multiple senses.* Show *and* tell. This is natural in dancing. Begin teaching a new pattern by showing what it is supposed to look like. Next, explain each of the steps in a way that is memorable. Dance the pattern again, while saying each of the steps; then, have the dancers move through the pattern. As the students practice, you will need to dance it with each of them to help them learn what it feels like when it is correct.

6. *Phrase instructions to emphasize desired behaviors and be specific when giving correction.* The brain has difficulty processing negative information. "Don't take a heel lead," doesn't give information about what to do, instead. Instructions are easier to follow if you tell someone what *to* do, rather than what *not* to do. The more clear you are in giving instruction about how to improve, the easier it will be for the student to comply. "Show more rhythm" is too vague. "Lift your left hip higher as you step back on two" is much easier to execute because it is specific. Show and tell.

7. *Break instructional material into small chunks.* One of the most common complaints from adults taking beginning dance classes is that too much material is taught. Dancing is a complex skill. Once you have developed a high level of skill, it can be hard to remember what it felt like to be a beginner. Teach less material, and break it into small pieces so that students can experience mastery of some of the new material. Don't try to crowd too much into one dance lesson.

It is better for students to leave the class feeling confident that they can execute two patterns in the fox trot, for example, than to try to add in the rumba, even though, to you, it is clear that a rumba box and a fox trot box are basically the same. Wait until the next lesson; review; and only then, when you are sure they all got the fox trot box, show the students how they can use that box in the rumba.

8. *Teach to the level of the student.* In a group class this can be hard to do, but try to avoid giving either too much or too little information. If you show a new pattern with three possible endings, most students will find this confusing. Pick one version of the pattern and demonstrate only that. At the same time, be

sure to include all the essential information students need to execute the pattern.

9. *Provide positive reinforcement, as well as correction.* For example, "Good job! That's it! You've got it!" Positive reinforcement is important on two levels. It provides *information* about whether moves are being correctly executed, while also providing *reassurance.* People tend to be anxious about how they look to others, and dancing brings this anxiety out. Anxiety interferes with learning. People worry about how others are evaluating them instead of focusing on what they are doing. Positive reinforcement gives informational guidance while reducing anxiety.

10. *Review and repeat.* Begin every lesson with a review of material taught in previous lessons. Repeat information as needed throughout the lesson when you see that students do not understand the material. Of course you will advise everyone to practice, but only the most serious students will actually practice outside of the class or private lesson. Therefore, the review during the lesson is the only practice the average student is getting. If you move on to new material that assumes mastery of material already taught, students who do not get enough review will not be able to keep up, will become discouraged, and will quit.

11. *"Normalize" mistakes.* Too much focus on mistakes creates anxiety. Let students know that mistakes are an expected part of the learning process: "Everyone does this." "It took me a long time to learn this pattern."

12. *Be patient.* Expect to explain and demonstrate the same material over and over. Students who are slow learners represent job security for you. Smile and show it again, willingly. Reward the courage shown when a student asks a question. "I'm so glad you asked. I forgot to mention... Thanks."

13. *Be unfailingly polite.* Rudeness or brusqueness chills the atmosphere for everyone in the studio and drives students away. You want them to tell their friends how much fun it is.

14. *Be a positive role model.* Through your demeanor and behavior, you are showing students what it is like to be a dancer. Whether you or they are aware of it, students will tend to copy other aspects of your behavior, not just your dancing. Be the kind of dancer you want your students to be.

Note: There is a huge body of writing based on research in human learning. The above represents just a small taste. If you want to read more about principles of effective teaching, you might want to pick up a copy of *Powerful Principles of Instruction,* by Stephen L. Yelon.

Made in the USA
Lexington, KY
18 December 2014